PRECISION BRIDGE
for EVERYONE

By *Chas. H. Goren*

and **C. C. WEI**

A CHANCELLOR HALL *Book*
DOUBLEDAY & COMPANY, INC.
GARDEN CITY, N.Y.

Contents

Acknowledgement

MANY PEOPLE HAVE contributed to the development of the Precision System, and to its presentation for use by the casual bridge partnerships or by comparative newcomers to bridge competition. Foremost among those who helped on this book, however, and deserving of special acknowledgement and thanks, is Ron Andersen, the Precision star who won the 1977 McKenney Trophy awarded to the player who earns the most ACBL Master Points in a single year.

In achieving this, Ron shattered the record set only one year before and became the first player in history to win more than 2,000 master points in a tournament year — more than many great stars have accumulated in an entire bridge career. In addition to star performances in the four National Championships, this entailed winning more than 30 Regional titles (many of them as the partner of Kathryn Wei, who broke a long-standing drought among East Coast women stars by finishing fourth in the McKenney). It is amazing, therefore, that Ron found time to do a considerable share in the preparation of material presented in this book, and the authors are duly grateful.

Charles H. Goren   *C. C. Wei*

CHARLES H. GOREN

No, this is not the announcement of major changes in the Goren methods that have become known as Standard American — the most widely played system in the world and therefore the easiest to play in any game even with strangers as partners.

But I am mindful of what happened to the Culbertson System when Ely refused to recognize the virtues of point count until it was too late. He said, "Bridge players aren't going to take their shoes off to count beyond ten," referring to the fact that there were fewer than ten honor tricks in any deal, whereas there were always 40 High Card Points.

I am not going to make the error of underestimating the ability of the bridge-playing public, or of trying to predict what they will never do. Some half century ago, David Burnstine wrote a book advocating an opening bid of two clubs to show a big hand. The book didn't become a best-seller and the artificial two club opening, although it was almost immediately adopted by leading experts, has yet to be accepted by a vast majority of the players who play at home, or even in the small-city clubs. Nevertheless, it is in my book* and I have played it for years myself.

Weak two-bids, and recently weak jump overcalls, have become widely used in upper bridge circles, and they, too, are in my book. Nevertheless, in most games the simple announcement, "Everything strong," gets new partnerships off to a flying start with a minimum of discussion.

Five-card majors are now taught by some "Goren" teachers. I have not adopted them, but neither have I excommunicated those teachers who recommend the method. And they are in my book.

---

* *Goren's Bridge Complete*

In the book's more recent editions, I have recommended and described C. C. Wei's Precision Club method as the best system for players who want to try a forcing one club bid. It would be ostrich-like to ignore a system that has become the second-most popular method among duplicate and tournament players; indeed, I wrote my own book about Precision† more than seven years ago.

Since then, Precision has been modified — though not always simplified. Recently, C. C. Wei, recognizing the importance of making Precision easier for everyone, invited me to collaborate in this project. I was planning to expand the coverage of the Precision System in my forthcoming revision of Goren Complete, so I am delighted to accept his invitation.

If certain aspects of "Standard American" are causing you difficulty, you might find Precision smooths your problems. C. C. Wei's introduction will tell you why he believes that it will.

March, 1978

---

† *Chas. H. Goren presents "THE PRECISION SYSTEM."*

Introduction

C. C. WEI

First, I must thank Charles Goren for collaborating in this book. I heartily agree that Precision is a system for those who find certain aspects of Standard American troublesome. Precision is a natural system, based on the Goren Point Count, and the transition from Standard American to Precision can easily be made bit by bit. Many of those who head their convention cards "Standard American" are already using portions of Precision: not opening four-card major suits, to give just a single example.

When first I set about constructing the Precision System, it was with the idea of making bridge more enjoyable by making the bidding easier and at the same time more accurate. I am a trained engineer, a ship-builder and a mathematician. Also, I love bridge. So I spent several years analyzing what was difficult about Standard American and how it could profitably be simplified.

First, there was this huge hole through which so many points escaped: the fact that an opening bid in a suit had far too wide a range — from a floor of 13 HCP (sometimes, with good distribution, as few as 12 or even 11) to a ceiling of 20-22. Opener's partner always strained to keep the bidding open with 6 or even 5 and yet his one-over-one response was almost unlimited, so that before the partnership could sign off, they had gotten too high. Yet, if responder elected to be conservative and pass partner's one-bid, that seemed always to be the time when opener held the big hand and game could be made — perhaps in a different declaration.

The long-time world champion Italian team had solved this problem by opening hands of 17 points or more with a bid of one club. The idea was sound. If opener bid anything but one club, no matter how strongly he bid thereafter, his partner knew he could not have as many as 17 HCP. But mathematical calculations convinced me that the bottom level was too high and that 16 points not only was the crucial minimum but occurred just about twice as often. So if there was value to showing a strong hand with the first bid, there must be twice as much value in being able to use it twice as often.

Next, there was the obstacle of finding the right opening bid when a player had two or even three four-card suits to choose from. Precision took care of this by moving the one notrump range back to 13-15 HCP on balanced hands. If partner sought a fit in a four-card major, he could discover it by a Stayman two club response. Naturally, then, an opening bid in a major suit should be at least five cards in length and partner could raise with no misgivings even if he had only three-card support.

What did we do on the kind of balanced 16-18 point hand that was formerly opened one notrump? Simple: we opened with one club and rebid one notrump. This served to tighten up the whole notrump range, as you will see a little later.

In Standard American, the only limited bids are notrump openings. In Precision, all opening bids are limited except the opening bid of one club. And, as everyone who plays bridge knows, the first limited bid in the auction usually tells partner how high he can safely go.

I am not going to try to teach you the entire Precision System in this introduction. I am merely citing a few of the reasons why Precision is both simpler and more precise.

Since the primary purpose of Precison was to make rubber bridge easier for beginners and average players, I was gratified to find it so widely adopted (and adapted) by top-flight players everywhere. True, hey added a few — in some cases, many — conventions of their own intil gradually Precision in the hands of the experts became something ither than the simple route to better bidding that I had set out to create.

And that is the reason for this book. It is aimed at putting *precision* — NOT complication — into *your* game. Try out just a few of its conventions and see if it does not make your bidding so much easier and more accurate that soon your friends will be clamoring for you to teach it to them. If you don't want to teach, you can always suggest that they buy a copy of this book. Or, better still, give them one.

March, 1978

Chapter 1

Bidding Precisely

BIDDING PRECISELY is simply a matter of knowing the Precision "language" and then communicating effectively. Since Precision is a very natural bidding system, you'll find most of the "language" similar to what you already use playing standard methods. Except that the "language" has now become so simple and precise that your partnership is off to a quick and efficient start. The best way to learn is to do so with a favorite partner. But you can play with any Precision partner with no fear of misunderstandings.

However, even before the auction starts it is important to understand completely a few principles that are an important part of all openings, responses, and rebids. These principles are vital in hitting the Precision targets: Where? and How High? — the questions all Precision auctions are designed to answer quickly. Consequently, we shall review them before we consider the specific meaning of various bids and responses.

Counting Points

Precision uses the conventional approach of counting points to determine the value of your hand with a few important modifications. First, High Card Points (HCP) are counted in the standard Goren fashion used by most of the world's players — novice and expert alike.

Ace: 4
King: 3
Queen: 2
Jack: 1

In Precision, you consider only High Card Points in opening the bidding. When you raise (or plan to raise) your partner's suit, you should add to your High Card Points what we shall term Distribution Points (DP) as follows:

Void: 5
Singleton: 3
Doubleton: 1

The total of your HCP and DP will give responder the number of Supporting Points the hand contains for *raising partner's suit*. Remember, however, you only count Distribution Points (whether you are the opener or the responder) when raising partner's suit, not when you open or plan to introduce a new suit in the bidding.

Because Distribution Points may or may not become a factor depending on the auction, your total point count may change during the auction. For example, suppose that you are the dealer and hold:

♠ K J 10 4   ♡ A Q 10 9 5   ◇ Q 10 9   ♣ 3

Your hand is worth a total of 12 High Card Points (four for the ace, three for the king, two for each of the two queens, and one for the jack); you don't count any DP since you are not raising your partner's suit. (In fact, he hasn't even bid yet.) But when you hold a five-card or longer suit you may sometimes open with as few as 11 points!

Let's say you open the bidding 1 ♡ and partner responds 1 ♠. You certainly intend to raise his suit with such good support, so you must now add your Distribution Points to your High Card Points to determine your supporting strength. In the example you would be able to add 3 points (equal to the high card value of a king) for your singleton club — and your hand is now worth 15 points. Note that your hand improves in strength (from 12 to 15) when a good suit fit with partner is found.

Should partner respond 2 ♣ over your 1 ♡ opening, the value of your hand remains at 12 points. You have absolutely no intention of raising clubs with such terrible suport so you cannot add any DP to your 12 HCP. As a matter of fact, unless you can locate a fit in another suit, your club shortness is probably a liability since clubs is likely to be partner's longest suit and he is suggesting it as a possible trump suit.

The primary merit in using point count is its simplicity and universal use. It is very effective, particularly in notrump bidding or when an excellent trump suit has been established, in giving you a reasonable prediction of your side's trick-taking potential. During the bidding both partners should keep clearly in mind the following KEY NUMBERS that act as a general guide to the number of tricks you are likely to take and whether you are in part score, game, or slam territory.

Less than 25 points: Stop at a part score.

25 points: Strength usually required to be worth a game bid in notrump or a major suit. (3NT/4 ♡/4 ♠)

29 points: Minimum strength usually required to produce game in a minor suit. (5 ♣/5 ◊)

33 points: Minimum strength usually required to produce a small slam (12 tricks). (6 ♣/6 ◊/6 ♡/6 ♠/6NT)

37 points: Minimum strength usually required to produce a grand slam (13 tricks). (7 ♣/7 ◊/7 ♡/7 ♠/7NT)

However, no one, including Lloyd's of London, will insure that you will be able to make a game every time in a major suit with a good fit and 25 points, or a small slam with 33 points and a good fit. These KEY NUMBERS should be viewed only as barometers or general gauges — one need only consider the bum steers of the local weatherman to comprehend the fallibility of gauges and barometers. Nonetheless, as a general rule these key numbers will serve you well in determining the relative trick-taking potential of your combined hands.

Thus far, the only major difference between Precision and Standard American is that Distributional Points for doubletons, singletons and voids are counted only when you raise partner's suit.

Evaluating Your Hand Precisely

Although the backbone of evaluating your hand is the point count approach, it is by no means the only thing to consider. To be a good bidder you must realize that the value of your hand is constantly changing and depends on many factors including:

The importance of having your honors concentrated in your long suits rather than your short suits. For example, it is far better to hold:

(a)   ♠ A K 7 6 2   ♡ A Q 10 9 8   ◊ 5 4   ♣ 3

than to hold:

(b)   ♠ 9 8 6 5 3   ♡ A 8 4 3 2   ◊ A Q   ♣ K

Even though both hands have the same distributional pattern and exact high cards, (a) is likely to produce far more tricks than (b).

How well your hands "fit" together.

The amount of support you have for partner's long suits as well as your honors being located in the "right" places to cover his losers. To illustrate:

♠ K Q 9 7   ♡ A J 10 7 3 2   ◊ Q 10   ♣ 4

As the dealer, you open 1 ♡ on this minimum 12 count. Partner responds 1 ♠. Already your hand is better. You raise to 2 ♠ with your fine four-card support and partner bids 3 ◊. All of a sudden your queen of diamonds, which was a doubtful value, becomes a fine card. Your minimum opening bid has turned into a good, useful one with all its values working. You have excellent trump support, two valuable side suit controls* (the ace of hearts and singleton club), and a useful Q 10 doubleton in partner's second suit. As we shall further discuss later, you should promptly jump to game in spades, informing partner of your improved hand. There is no danger that partner will overestimate the value of your hand because you cannot have as many as 16 HCP. (Already, the value of opening 1 ♣ on all hands of 16 or more is making itself felt.) For now, however, the important thing is that you realize how well your hands "fit" together. Consider how different our evaluation of the hand's worth would be if partner responds 2 ♣ over our 1 ♡ opening. After our 2 ♡ rebid, partner calls 3 ◊ — just what we didn't want to hear. We have a total of only three cards in partner's long suits. However, responder's rebid of a new suit, especially a higher-ranking suit (a reverse) is forcing and we must bid again. Probably our only choice is to bid 3NT — we have already shown six hearts and we do have spade strength. But thus far the bidding indicates that the hand is a misfit, and misfits should be devalued. There is no suit that is an obvious source of a number of tricks, and we may be in trouble unless partner was preparing to give a delayed raise in hearts — a sequence that is more likely in Standard American than in Precision.

The possible "positional" value of an honor or high honors in combination.

Sometimes honors will increase or decrease in value during the auction due to your opponent's bidding as well as partner's calls. Suppose you hold ♠AQ3 and your *right-hand* opponent introduces spades in the auction. Your ace-queen in that suit may take on the stature of the ace-king in the likely event that your right-hand opponent holds the ♠ K.

---

*The ability to win the first or second round of a suit.

Conversely, should your *left-hand* opponent bid spades when you have the same holding, the value of the ♠ Q diminishes considerably because the likelihood is that the ♠ K will capture your ♠ Q. Keep in mind the following simple maxim in competitive auctions: "If your honors are located behind your opponent's strength they increase in value, and if they are located in front of likely enemy strength their value decreases. In addition, unsupported jacks and queens in your opponents' suit should usually be heavily discounted because they are unlikely to produce any tricks.

The importance of "communication" in the play of the hand.

Although the strength required to produce 3NT is approximately 25 points, it is far easier to produce the necessary nine tricks when the partnership's assets are divided 12 opposite 13 than with 22 points in declarer's hand and 3 in the dummy. The reason is simple: declarer's ability to lead up to strength often makes several tricks difference in the play. When the points are more evenly divided, several entries usually exist to both hands, giving declarer options in playing various suits and establishing tricks.

The presence of Quick Tricks

Before the Goren 4-3-2-1 point count method, bridge players evaluated their hands primarily in terms of honor count. This is still a valuable aid in determining the defensive worth of a hand. Using this approach, usually called either quick tricks or defensive tricks, the following basic scale is employed:

A-K	2	K-Q	1
A-Q	1½	K-x	½
A	1	Q-J-10	½*

Strong bids guarantee and high contracts demand a reasonable number of quick tricks, because these represent cards that will prevent the opponents from immediately winning two or three tricks in a suit. You cannot hope to score game contracts without control cards.

Quick tricks are useful not only in the play if your side gets the bid, but also in defense should the enemy play the hand. So that partner can evaluate his hand both offensively and defensively, a typical Precision opening bid (other than 1 ♣ as you will learn) implies at least *two quick tricks.*

---

*But only in a short suit, or in the opponents' trump suit.)

The ability and experience of you and your partner.

There are, of course, other factors that an experienced player takes into account: The comparative skill of your partner and your opponents; the potency of the liquid refreshments, and how this affects the individual players; even the superstitions that they entertain. We don't really believe that "the cards always run in the same direction of the bathtub." But if YOU believe it, it will be best to play in a house that has two bathtubs that don't run the same way.

The fact is that there is more to evaluating your hand and bidding precisely than simply counting points. POINTS DON'T TAKE TRICKS, as the Duke of Cumberland learned in Bath, England, some 200 years ago, when his opponents made a grand slam in clubs against the West hand in the famous deal recorded in several bridge anthologies:

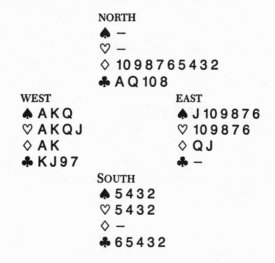

```
                    NORTH
                    ♠ —
                    ♡ —
                    ◇ 10 9 8 7 6 5 4 3 2
                    ♣ A Q 10 8
    WEST                            EAST
    ♠ A K Q                         ♠ J 10 9 8 7 6
    ♡ A K Q J                       ♡ 10 9 8 7 6
    ◇ A K                           ◇ Q J
    ♣ K J 9 7                       ♣ —
                    SOUTH
                    ♠ 5 4 3 2
                    ♡ 5 4 3 2
                    ◇ —
                    ♣ 6 5 4 3 2
```

The Duke was playing whist, the forerunner of bridge, where there was a trump suit on every hand, sometimes determined by a turned card. The bet was that the Duke would not take a trick against a club contract. In accordance with sound whist practice when holding a strong (!) hand, the Duke led a low trump to limit an opposing crossruff. Unfortunately for the Duke, this lead allowed the scoundrels sitting North-South to win all thirteen tricks.

(Win the ♣8, ruff a diamond, finesse the ♣10, ruff another diamond, finesse the ♣Q, cash the ♣A and the diamonds are good.) Though this deal was so obviously contrived that it should not have taken in even the son of a king whose folly was to cost England its American colonies, it does illustrate that point count doesn't always succeed in determining the trick-taking potential of a hand. Remember, the "perfect" bridge hand (holding a 13 card suit) contains only 10 High Card Points.

We are now ready to move from hand evaluation, the individual player's concern, to the language of bidding, the aspect that converts bridge into a partnership game. Basically, bidding is what bridge is all about, and Precision bidding is the most easily intelligible bridge language.

Chapter 2

Hitting the Precision Targets
WHERE? HOW HIGH?

GOOD BIDDING is merely a simple exchange of information attempting to answer two questions: Where? How High? If you and your partner are able to answer both of these questions accurately most of the time, you will have mastered just about all you need to know about effective communication at the bridge table.

Note that we did not just say *you*, but you and your partner. Being able to communicate successfully during the auction is primarily a matter of knowing and using the same precise "language" as your partner. Your target is the best final contract for the *partnership*. Bidding precisely is nothing more than good communication with a highly specialized, simple language packed into 15 words. As in all good communication, you must learn to be a good *listener* as well as an effective, direct speaker.

How high? — the limited bid strategy

The limited bid strategy, used by all good players regardless of system, is the key to Precision bidding. It means simply this: If your partner makes a bid that defines his point-count and distribution very precisely (which we call a limited bid), you should add your points to his and then determine your chances for game or slam. If you find that your side *cannot* hold the minimum number of points required to bid game (summarized on page 11), stop at a low-level playable part-score contract. If you *may* have the required strength to bid game but you cannot be sure, invite partner to go on to game if he has a maximum for his previous bidding, letting him make the final decision. Finally, if your side *must* have the values for game, make certain that game is reached — either by bidding it yourself or by making a forcing bid that partner cannot pass. The same is true if you are fortunate enough to hold adequate strength to place your partnership in slam territory.

In practice, the limited bid strategy is far simpler than it may sound.

Example 1: Suppose partner opens the bidding with 1NT and you hold the following hand, worth 10 High Card Points:

♠ K 7 6   ♡ A 8 6   ◇ J 10 3 2   ♣ Q 10 4

If you are using standard Goren methods, partner's 1NT opening shows 16-18 HCP and a balanced hand. Since the opening bid limits partner's hand very precisely in terms of both strength and distribution, you add your points to his and determine that your partnership has somewhere between 26 and 28 HCP. Thus, game should be bid and slam is out of reach, so you end the auction by raising to 3NT — surely the best contract since both hands are balanced and no eight card major suit fit exists.

Example 2: Holding the same hand (♠ K 7 6   ♡ A 8 6   ◇ J 10 3 2   ♣ Q 10 4), you are using the Precision system, so partner's opening bid shows 13-15 HCP and a balanced hand. What should you bid? Even though we haven't discussed the Precision 1NT bid, you should find it easy to solve this problem by using the limited bid strategy. When you add your 10 points to partner's 13-15 points, you discover the total for the partnership is somewhere between 23 and 25 HCP. Therefore, your side will have the required strength for game ony if partner has a maximum 1NT opening (15 HCP), not if he holds less. Consequently, you should invite game by raising to 2NT which partner will pass with a minimum or raise to game with a maximum.

Example 3: With a slightly weaker hand (♠ K 7 6 ♡ A 8 6◇ J 10 3 2 ♣ J 10 4), knowing that partner's Precision 1NT opening bid shows 13-15 HCP with balanced distribution, what call should you make? Adding your 9 HCP to partner's 13-15, you know that your partnership can have no more than 24 HCP and may have as few as 22. Since your side cannot have game-going strength or an eight card major suit fit, you should pass 1NT.

The simple mathematics illustrated in these examples is made possible by the limited opening bid of 1NT, which precisely defines partner's point count and distribution.

Unfortunately, situations such as our illustrations are rare in standard bidding *except* when the opening bid is 1NT. Most standard opening bids are relatively unlimited in terms of strength or distribution: An opening bid of one of a suit may be made with as little as a balanced 12 or

13 count or with as much as a 21 or 22 point powerhouse that does not quite meet the specifications for a strong two-bid. This huge range of possibilities often causes difficult problems in subsequent bidding, not only for the opener but also the responder as well. Because the Precision range for all natural opening suit bids is strictly limited (11 to 15 HCP), subsequent bidding is much easier to handle. What sets this limit? The fact that opener did not begin with 1 ♣.

Where?

"Where" to play a hand will often depend on whether the combined partnership strength indicates the values for a part score, game, or slam. When the limit of the hand is a part score, safety is the most important consideration. As you know from the scoring system, there is no real advantage in bidding a major suit part score instead of a minor suit or 2NT instead of two of a suit when game is out of reach. Scoring an extra 10, 20, or 30 points does not warrant any risk unless it is enough to complete a previous part score, thus making game. Therefore, you should always try to play your part score contracts with your longest combined suit as trump or in some low number of notrump if this seems safe when no good fit exists.

When you and your partner hold sufficient values for game, your problems are a bit more complicated. Safety, of course, is still the watchword, but game possibilities, with their accompanying rewards on the score sheet, usually warrant more exploration.

Poor bidders overwork 3NT as their vehicle for game. They are primarily motivated by having to win only nine tricks rather than the ten or eleven required for suit games. On the surface this may seem reasonable, but what is overlooked is that suit contracts normally play at least one trick better than notrump contracts when you have a good combined trump suit. This is frequently dramatized at the bridge table watching a declarer at a notrump contract helplessly discarding high cards and long suit winners while one opponent cashes a running suit. Often a suit contract would have been iron-clad.

Because suit contracts are frequently safer, Precision always explores for an eight card or better major suit fit, whether the limit of the hand is a part score, game, or slam. With the values for game, before settling in 3NT or five of a minor, an intensive search should be conducted. If you find that your side owns a minimum of eight cards in a major suit, play the hand in four of that major. Occasionally, the stars will be so positioned as to doom your major suit game when 3NT would have come rolling home. In those rare instances you have our sympathy as well as your partner's. As we noted earlier, at the bridge table you can only hope to do those things that will work out most often. And most often it will be right to play 4 ♡ or 4 ♠ when you have the values for game and an eight card trump fit.

Lacking a major suit fit, if the combined hands possess stoppers in all four suits and the values for game, 3NT is usually the best contract.

Moving to diamonds and clubs, keep in mind that minor suit games require additional strength and controls since you must be able to win eleven of the thirteen tricks before the oponents take more than two. Usually we arrive at 5 ◊ or 5 ♣ after a process of elimination. We don't have a major suit fit, our hands are not suitable for notrump, but we do have ample strength and controls for game with our good fit in the minor suit.

Having now reached the lofty heights of the five level, we are only a short step away from the slam zone. Probably no greater thrill exists at the bridge table than bidding and making a slam. Nor is any bidding endeavor more challenging. Since slam bidding will be discussed later in this book, we give you only one bit of advice at this juncture: Never concern yourself with 100 honors or who will play the hand, or the extra few points for playing in notrump rather than a minor suit. When a bonus ranging from 500 to 1500 points is at stake, you always want to play in the safest slam possible.

Our final thoughts on "Where" and "How High" may seem inconsistent with the "scientific" approach to modern bidding, but bridge is not and never has been an exact science. At times you will be faced with hands and decisions not discussed, outlined, or charted in this or any other bridge book. There are times when no bid will exactly describe your hand. Who knows, for example, what the best action is with "freak" hands such as one containing an eleven card suit and two singletons? What is our solution to such problems where neither the system nor the limited bid strategy can help? It involves judgment and common sense. *Bid what you think you can make.* Fortunately, on the vast majority of hands that are likely to be dealt, Precision will provide an accurate "How High" and a precise "Where."

As you will learn, Precision improves your bidding by greatly increasing the number of limited opening bids at your disposal, which increases the frequency of the limited bid strategy. In Precision, opening bids of 1 ◊, 1 ♡, 1 ♠, 2 ♣, and 2 ◊ are all limited to the precise range of 11-15 HCP. The distributional possibilities are also limited. This major improvement is achieved simply by limiting opening bids in a major to at least five-card length, and by using a strong, forcing 1 ♣ opening bid to show a hand of 16 or more HCP, which will be the subject of our next chapter.

Chapter 3

The Precision Opening 1 ♣

THIS CHAPTER deals with those happy occasions when your hand is strong enough to open the bidding with a forcing 1 ♣ bid. It is the cornerstone of Precision bidding for two reasons: (1) 1 ♣ is the only *strong*, FORCING opening in the Precision System; and (2) It LIMITS all other opening bids (except 2NT) to a maximum of 15 High Card Points.

Opening 1 ♣
"The big gun in your Precision arsenal"

The Precision 1 ♣ opening bid promises 16 or more High Card Ponts. It does not guarantee any strength or length in clubs. Opening 1 ♣ simply says, "I have a good hand, and I'll tell you more about it at my next turn to bid. In the meantime, what does your hand look like, partner?"

Since the 1 ♣ opener may not have a club in his hand or might hold the values for a strong two-bid in any suit, partner must not pass even if he has a complete Yarborough. 1 ♣ is 100% FORCING. Remember, it is the only UNLIMITED opening bid in the system. In Precision, all hands with 16 or more High Card Points are opened 1 ♣, with one exception: As in standard bidding, hands with 22-24 HCP and balanced distribution are opened 2NT.

Consider your opening bid on the following examples:

(1) ♠ K Q 10 9 5   ♡ A Q 10 8   ◇ A J 9 3   ♣ —

Open 1 ♣. You have the required 16 HCP.

(2) ♠ K Q J 2   ♡ A K Q J 10   ◇ A   ♣ A K J

Open 1 ♣. There is no UPPER limit to the 1 ♣ opening. With this 28-point "mountain" it is your only forcing bid.

(3)   ♠ A Q   ♡ –   ◇ K J 10 9 5   ♣ K Q 10 9 7 3

Open 1 ◇, not 1 ♣. Even though your playing strength is exceptional, you lack the required 16 HCP to open 1 ♣. As we shall discuss later, strong rebids are available to describe excellent distributional hands after a "limited" opening bid like 1 ◇.

(4)   ♠ K Q 10 6   ♡ A K J   ◇ K Q 9   ♣ A J 3

Open 2NT, not 1 ♣. A perfect description of your balanced 23 count.

As example (3) illustrates, we consider only High Card Points in determining whether to open the bidding and what to open. Distributional Points (as you will recall from Chapter 1) are counted *only* when you raise (or are planning to raise) partner's suit.

Responding to 1 ♣

When partner opens 1 ♣ and you are the responder, you have four tools at your disposal to describe your hand.

(1) The Negative 1 ◇ response (for hands with less than 8 HCP);

(2) A Positive Suit response (promising 8 or more HCP and at least a five-card suit);

(3) A Positive Notrump response (for balanced hands with 8 or more HCP); and

(4) The Unusual Positive response (with 8 or more HCP and specifically 4-4-4-1 distribution).

No bid in the auction is more critical in directing the partnership to the best final contract than the initial response to a 1 ♣ opening. Consequently, we shall consider in turn each of the four types of responses.

The negative 1 ◇ response

When partner opens 1 ♣ and you have a weak hand, your most important obligation is to flash a warning signal to partner immediately. Responding 1 ◇ informs the 1 ♣ opener that you have from 0-7 HCP and that caution is in order, even though he holds a fine hand. This negative response does not promise any strength or length in diamonds, just as partner's 1 ♣ opening said nothing about his club holding; 1 ◊ simply says, "I'm sorry, I have a pretty bad hand so take it easy. Tell me more about your good hand and I'll let you know more about mine with my second bid."

For example, if partner opens 1 ♣, respond 1 ◊ with any of the following hands:

(1) ♠ 5 4 3 2   ♡ 4 3 2   ◊ 4 3 2   ♣ 4 3 2

You cannot pass! Partner may hold a strong two-bid in diamonds, hearts, or spades without a club in his hand.

(2) ♠ Q J 10 9 5 2   ♡ 5   ◊ 7   ♣ Q 10 9 6 5

You'll show your suits later; the first order of business is to warn partner that you have less than 8 HCP.

(3) ♠ J 10 7   ♡ A Q 10 9 3   ◊ 7 6 4 2   ♣ 8

Although this is a maximum negative response, you have no other choice than to respond 1 ◊ initially. Remember, you consider only HCP unless you are raising partner's suit, so at this point you cannot add any Distribution Points to your 7 HCP.

Once responder has limited his high card strength by responding 1 ◊, he is free to describe both his distribution and whether he has a maximum negative (6 or 7 HCP) such as example (3), or a minimum 1 ◊ response (0-5 HCP), perhaps as bad as our disastrous (1). Although subsequent bidding by both the opener and responder is completely natural, responder has denied holding as many as 8 HCP and the opener has promised at least 16. Therefore, both opener and responder are free to pass a low-level rebid if the proposed contract is playable and game is out of reach. The only exception is when opener describes a strong two-bid with his rebid, in which case the partnership is forced to game.

Positive suit responses
1 ♡ - 1 ♠ - 2 ♣ - 2 ◊

With 8 or more HCP and a long suit of five or more cards, announce the good news to partner by bidding your longest suit. (If your suit happens to be diamonds you are forced to respond 2 ◊ since 1 ◊ is reserved for the negative response.) When you are blessed with two long suits of equal length (both at least five-cards long), bid the higher ranking suit first as you would using standard methods.

Let's consider a few examples. Partner opens 1 ♣ and you hold:

(1)   ♠ A K Q J   ♡ 10 9 5 3 2   ◇ J 10 6   ♣ 4

Respond 1 ♡. Do not be concerned about the relative weakness of your heart suit compared to the powerful four-card spade suit. Bidding 1 ♡ promises only that you have at least five hearts and a minimum of 8 HCP. It does not necessarily suggest that your points are in the heart suit, but merely that you have at least 8 of them somewhere.

(2)   ♠ K 10 9   ♡ 10 9 4   ◇ A Q 10 7 5 4   ♣ Q

Respond 2 ◇. Since 1 ◇ is simply negative, you must bid 2 ◇ to show you have a positive response and a diamond suit.

(3)   ♠ K Q J 10 6 2   ♡ A K 10 4   ◇ Q 10   ♣ 5

Respond 1 ♠. Opener must bid again, and you will be able to show your great strength as the bidding progresses. Remember, a positive suit response is UNLIMITED. You could have as many as 24 HCP. (If you ever pick up more than 24 when partner opens 1 ♣, you might as well throw the hand in since you are no doubt playing with a defective deck!)

(4)   ♠ Q 9   ♡ A 10 9 4   ◇ 6 5   ♣ Q 10 8 3 2

Respond 2 ♣. Keep in mind that you cannot count any Distribution Points even though both partner and you have bid clubs — his 1 ♣ bid did not show a suit so you are not raising. Making a positive response in one suit does not preclude holding one or even two four-card side suits.

(5)   ♠ K Q J 10 7   ♡ J 10 8 7 3   ◇ 4   ♣ 10 9

Respond 1 ◇. You only hold 7 HCP. If you held another jack you should respond 1 ♠ with your 5-5 distribution, irrespective of the strength of the suits.

Since the opener holds upwards of 16 HCP and responder has a minimum of 8 for a positive response, the partnership's prospects for game are excellent. Therefore, with very few exceptions that we shall discuss later in this chapter a positive response forces both opener and responder to keep the bidding open until a playable game contract is reached. Neither opener nor responder is forced to jump in subsequent bidding simply to insure that partner will not pass. Jumps can be reserved to describe exceptional distributional features or pinpoint specific strength.

If the 1 ◊ response is viewed as a flashing yellow signal (advising caution), then a positive suit response can properly be considered a bright green light. Game is more than likely, and the partnership should have a smooth ride in reaching the best final contract.

Positive notrump responses
1NT-2NT-3NT

If you have 8 or more High Card Points but don't have a five-card or longer suit and your hand is balanced, a positive notrump response will perfectly describe your hand.* The following scale outlines the strength shown:

1NT: 8-10 HCP with balanced distribution
2NT: 11-13 HCP with balanced distribution
3NT: 14-15 HCP with balanced distribution

If responder is blessed with more than 15 HCP and a balanced hand, we usually advise responding 2NT and then bidding again after opener's rebid.

Using this scale, respond to a 1 ♣ opening with the following hands:

(1) ♠ A J 10 7   ♡ Q 10 9 5   ◊ J 10   ♣ 9 8 3

Respond 1 NT. A precise description of your balanced 8 HCP. As you will learn later in this chapter, if partner is interested in your major suit holdings he has the tools to inquire about them.

(2) ♠ K J 9   ♡ 6 5 4 3 2   ◊ A Q   ♣ Q J 10

Respond 1 ♡, not 2NT. Although you may elect to make a positive notrump response with a weak five-card *minor*, you should never make a notrump response with a five-card major.*

(3) ♠ K 10 9   ♡ K 10 4   ◊ 8 6 5 3 2   ♣ K 9

Respond 1NT. Although you hold five diamonds, it is best, with such a weak suit and honors scattered in the other suits, to bid 1NT.

---

*Balanced suit distribution includes all of the following: 4-3-3-3, 4-4-3-2, or 5-3-3-2 where the five-card suit is a relatively weak minor.

(4) ♠ A Q 10   ♡ K J 9 2   ◊ J 10   ♣ K 10 9 5

Respond 3NT. With partner's known minimum of 16 HCP, slam is a distinct possibility if he has anything extra. 3NT should place him in an excellent position to judge the limit of your combined assets, using the Limited Bid Strategy.

When responder makes a positive notrump response, opener knows just about everything there is to know about partner's hand. Frequently, by using the Limited Bid Strategy, he will be able to set the final contract immediately. If he has any further questions about responder's hand, simple tools are available that we will consider later in this chapter.

As you can see, both suit and notrump positive responses are entirely natural. With a good responding hand and a long suit, you simply bid your long suit; with a good balanced hand and no long suit, you respond in notrump according to your strength.

Unusual positive responses
2♡ - 2♠ - 3♣ - 3◊

The negative 1 ◊, positive suit, and positive notrump responses take care of all hands except a positive response with 4-4-4-1 distribution. Let's take a look at examples of this unusal specimen:

(a) ♠ 9   ♡ K Q 10 3   ◊ A J 10 7   ♣ J 9 8 2

(b) ♠ K J 10 8   ♡ 8   ◊ K Q 5 4   ♣ Q 10 9 5

(c) ♠ J 10 8 4   ♡ A Q J 3   ◊ 5   ♣ K 8 7 5

(d) ♠ Q 8 4 2   ♡ K 9 7 6   ◊ A K Q 10   ♣ J

If partner opens 1♣, you certainly have the values for a positive response with any of these hands, but you cannot respond in notrump because your hand is unbalanced (you have a singleton), and you cannot bid a suit that is less than five cards in length. What can you bid?

The solution is what we call the Unusual Positive, which is one of the most distinctive and useful responses to the Precision ♣ opening. Here is how it works: You would really like to show partner all three of your four-card suits at once — and you can! Tell partner your exact distribution by JUMPING IN YOUR SINGLETON SUIT. (With diamonds you must *double* jump since 2 ◊ is a regular positive response.) In the examples, you would respond 2 ♠ with (a), 2 ♡ with (b), 3 ◊ with (c) and 3 ♣ with (d). It may seem a bit unusual to jump in your shortest suit, but you are actually showing the other three suits simultaneously.

After hearing your Unusual Positive response, partner will know that you have 8 or more HCP and a singleton in the suit you have just bid with precisely four cards in each of the other suits. In effect, you have, with one bid, shown excellent support for three potential trump suits giving the 1 ♣ opener an easy time in handling subsequent bidding.

Here are a few more examples. Partner opens 1 ♣ and you hold:

(1) ♠ K 9 8 2   ♡ A J 8 6   ◊ 5   ♣ 10 9 7 4

Respond 3 ◊. A 1 ◊ response would be negative, and 2 ◊ would be a regular positive suit response promising five or more diamonds. So you must bid 3 ◊ to describe your 4-4-1-4 distribution and game-going values.

(2) ♠ 8 6 4 3 2   ♡ –   ◊ A Q 10 5   ♣ K J 7 6

Respond 1 ♠, not 2 ♡. Remember, the Unusual Positive shows specifically 4-4-4-1 distribution. It cannot be used when your distribution is 5-4-4-0 since then you have a suit to bid as a regular positive response.

(3) ♠ 2   ♡ K Q J 10   ◊ A Q 10 5   ♣ A 8 5 3

Respond 2 ♠. Although your 16 HCP strongly suggests at least a small slam, first describe your distribution with the Unusual Positive response. Subsequently, you will describe your exceptional strength. As with the regular positive suit response, there is no upper limit to the HCP you can hold when you use the Unusual Positive.

(4) ♠ K 10 9 5   ♡ K 4 3 2   ◊ J 10 9 5   ♣ 10

Respond 1 ◊, not 3 ♣. You MUST hold 8 HCP for the Unusual Positive response, even when your distribution is otherwise perfect.

While a little memory work is involved in mastering the Unusual Positive response, you'll find that it will become easy and fun in no time. Any jump response to 1 ♣ should remind you that this is unusual. And, after all, how often at the bridge table will you be able to profit from the unique opportunity to show three specific suits with a single response?

Summarizing the Initial Responses to 1♣

Before proceeding further, let's summarize the responses to the 1♣ opening bid:

1◇	NEGATIVE. 0-7 High Card Points, any distribution.
1♡, 1♠, 2♣, 2◇	POSITIVE SUIT RESPONSE. 8 or more High Card Points, five or more cards in the bid suit.
1NT, 2NT, 3NT	POSITIVE NOTRUMP RESPONSES. Balanced distribution. 1NT: 8-10 HCP 2NT: 11-13 HCP 3NT: 14-15 HCP
2♡, 2♠, 3♣, 3◇	UNUSUAL POSITIVE RESPONSES. 8 or more High Card Points, 4-4-4-1 distribution with the singleton in the bid suit.

With the exception of 3NT, the 1♣ opener cannot pass any of these responses. He cannot pass 1◇ since responder may not have any diamonds in his hand, and he must not pass any of the forms of positive responses because game is very likely.

Keeping in mind the specific meaning of the bids available to the responder, let us move across the table and consider the various possibilities at opener's second turn to bid.

Rebids by the 1♣ opener

After a 1◇ response

If your 1♣ opening is greeted by a 1◇ response, you should proceed by making the most natural and descriptive bid possible. Do not forget, however, that partner has warned you that he holds a poor hand (no more than 7 HCP).

Should you hold a five-card or longer suit, simply bid it. (With two long suits of equal length, bid the higher ranking suit first, intending to rebid the other to give partner a convenient choice.) Responder may pass if game is out of the question and the contract is a playable one; otherwise, he will rebid naturally as his hand dictates. If you have a strong two-bid (defined as 22 points or 9 playing tricks) and want to insist that partner bid again, no matter how poor his hand is, jump in your long suit. The auction then continues as though you had opened the bidding with a standard Goren strong two-bid, except that the responder has already limited his strength to less than 8 HCP.

If you don't have a five-card or longer suit and your hand is balanced, rebid in notrump — bid 1NT with 16-18 HCP, 2NT with 19-21 HCP, and 3NT with 25-27 HCP. Responder can then follow your usual methods (Stayman,* etc.), including the Limited Bid Strategy. And of course he can even pass.

This leaves one difficult situation for us to consider. What does the 1 ♣ opener rebid when *he* has 4-4-4-1 distribution? He certainly cannot rebid any number of notrump, which promises a balanced hand, when he has a singleton. And rebidding in a suit technically guarantees at least five cards in the suit bid. The solution to this rare dilemma is that the opener must bid his cheapest four-card suit. Yes, partner will assume a five-card suit, but in practice this rarely creates any serious problems and it is the least of evils.

The following box outlines the methods we have been discussing:

Rebids by Opener after a 1 ◇ Response

Bid:	HCP:	Meaning:
1NT	16-18	Balanced hand
2NT	19-21	Balanced hand
3NT*	25-27	Balanced hand
1♡/1♠/2♣/2◇	16-21	Unbalanced; 5-card or longer suit**
2♡/2♠/3♣/3◇	22-up	(9+ playing tricks) Strong two-bid

*May include weak 5-card minor
**Exceptionally may include 4-4-4-1 distribution

---

*The Stayman Convention: 2 ♣ (or the cheapest bid in clubs over higher notrump rebids and openings) asks partner to bid a four-card major if he has one and bid 2 ◇ if he does not. With two four-card majors, responder should bid hearts first.

Using these methods, let us consider a few examples:

(A)	OPENER	RESPONDER
	♠ A Q 10 4	♠ J 5 3
	♡ K J 7	♡ Q 9 2
	◊ K Q 8 5	◊ J 10 7
	♣ K 10	♣ 9 8 4 2

Precision bidding:

1 ♣[1]	1 ◊[2]
1NT[3]	Pass[4]

[1] 16 or more HCP.
[2] Negative, 0-7 HCP.
[3] "I have a strong (16-18 HCP) balanced hand."
[4] "My hand is balanced and the Limited Bid Strategy indicates we lack the strength for game even if you have a maximum."

(B)	OPENER	RESPONDER
	♠ K Q 10 4	♠ J 9 5 3
	♡ A K 4	♡ Q 10 8 7
	◊ A J 10 5	◊ K 8
	♣ K 3	♣ 8 7 4

Precision bidding:

1 ♣	1 ◊
2NT[1]	3 ♣[2]
3 ♠[3]	4 ♠[4]

[1] 19-21 HCP, balanced hand.
[2] The Stayman Convention. With 6 HCP opposite a minimum of 19 in opener's hand, responder knows that game must be reached, so he tries to locate a 4-4- major suit fit. He plans to raise 3 ♡ or 3 ♠ to game or bid 3NT over 3 ◊.
[3] Four-card spade suit.
[4] As planned. The 4 ♠ contract is odds-on to make when 3NT could easily fail.

(C)	OPENER	RESPONDER
	♠ A Q 2	♠ J 10 7 5 4 3
	♡ A 10 7 5	♡ 4
	◊ K Q 10	◊ 8 7 3
	♣ Q 8 6	♣ 10 7 4

Precision bidding:

1 ♣	1 ◇
1NT	2 ♠[1]
Pass[2]	

[1] "Sorry partner, I have a very poor unbalanced hand with no interest in game. 2♠ should play better than 1NT."
[2] Respecting partner's sign-off.

(D)	OPENER	RESPONDER
	♠ A Q 10	♠ J 4 2
	♡ A K Q	♡ 10 9 8 4 3 2
	◇ K Q J 5	◇ 7
	♣ A 3 2	♣ 9 8 5

Precision bidding:

1 ♣	1 ◇
3NT[1]	4 ♡[2]
Pass[3]	

[1] 25-27 HCP, with a balanced hand.
[2] 4♡ should play much better than 3NT with my unbalanced hand, knowing we have a minimum of eight hearts in the combined hands.
[3] Nothing more to say.

(E)	OPENER	RESPONDER
	♠ A K J 10 6	♠ 9 8 2
	♡ A K 5	♡ Q 10 4 3
	◇ Q 10 7	◇ 7 6 4
	♣ 8 6	♣ 5 3 2

Precision bidding:

1 ♣	1 ◇
1 ♠[1]	Pass[2]

[1] Natural and non-forcing; strongly suggesting at least five spades and 16-21 HCP. (The only reason opener wouldn't have five spades is the rare 4-1-4-4 distribution.)
[2] "Sorry partner, but I have a terrible hand and 1♠ is probably as good a contract as any other. I certainly don't want to be any higher."

(F)   OPENER   RESPONDER
      ♠ A 10 4   ♠ 5 3 2
      ♡ 4   ♡ K Q 10 9 3
      ◇ A Q J 8 5   ◇ 6
      ♣ K Q J 10   ♣ 9 8 6 5

Precision bidding:

1 ♣	1 ◇
2 ◇¹	2 ♡²
3 ♣³	Pass⁴

¹ Natural and non-forcing promising at least five diamonds. (Remember, opener is NOT raising diamonds; 1 ◇ simply said responder has 0-7 HCP; he might not have a diamond in his hand.)
² Excellent opportunity to show your good five-card heart suit without misleading partner regarding your strength. (You can't hold more than 7 HCP.)
³ Holding a singleton heart, opener suggests his second suit as trump.
⁴ "Game is unlikely and we have found a fit."

The early indication that there is considerable strength in one hand and limited values in the other is very helpful when the weaker hand contains a long suit but little high card strength. Playing Precision, there is no temptation to get too high on hands of this sort:

(G)   OPENER   RESPONDER
      ♠ 4   ♠ K J 10 8 6 2
      ♡ A Q 10 7 3   ♡ 4 2
      ◇ A Q 8   ◇ J 5
      ♣ A J 9 5   ♣ 7 6 3

Precision bidding:

1 ♣	1 ◇
1 ♡	1 ♠¹
2 ♣²	2 ♠³
Pass⁴	

¹ Although responder is not forced to bid after opener's non-forcing 1 ♡ rebid, he certainly wants to suggest his fine spade suit as trump.
² Since partner may only hold a five-card spade suit, with such poor support for spades opener suggests his second suit (clubs) as trump.

³ With poor support for either of partner's suits and a reasonably good six-card suit of his own, responder rebids his suit rather than taking a preference for either of opener's suits. (Note that responder's hand might not produce a trick for the opener but will surely take several tricks if spades are trump.)

⁴ Although opener has diamonds well-stopped for notrump, the hand is obviously a misfit, so he passes in what may very well be the last chance for a plus score for his side.

Players using standard methods would almost surely go overboard on this hand. The bidding would begin: 1 ♡ - 1 ♠, 2 ♣ - 2 ♠, and the opener would be tempted to take one more bid with his fine 17 count. This would not necessarily be wrong since responder could easily hold a good 8 or 9 count in a standard auction. As you can see, any contract beyond 2 ♠ is likely to fail.

Traditional methods may also miss the best final contract when the opening bidder has a strong two-suiter and the responder has a very weak hand and lacks support for the first suit. This type of hand is perfect for the Precision ♣.

(H)	OPENER	RESPONDER
	♠ A K 10 9 3	♠ 2
	♡ A Q J 10 4	♡ K 9 8 3
	◊ A 7	◊ J 5 4 2
	♣ 3	♣ 9 8 6 2

The opener has a good hand but by no stretch of the imagination a strong two-bid. The bidding using standard methods is likely to die at 1 ♠ with responder holding only 4 HCP and a singleton in partner's suit.

Playing Precision, this type of deal presents no problems. Our bidding would simply go:

OPENER	RESPONDER
1 ♣	1 ◊
1 ♠¹	1NT²
3 ♡³	4 ♡⁴

¹ With two five-card suits opener shows the higher ranking suit first.

² Searching for a better contract, responder rebids 1NT describing moderate values and no fit for spades. (Obviously he hopes that opener will introduce a second suit which responder will like far better than spades.)

³ Non-forcing (since opener has denied holding a strong two-bid with his

initial 1♠ rebid), but highly invitational. Responder is urged to bid game in either of opener's suits.
4 Responder happily accepts opener's invitation to continue on to game. With four trump, the singleton in partner's first suit is no longer a liability but has turned into an asset.

When the opener holds an exceptionally strong hand, equal to a forcing two-bid, and responder bids 1◊, the bidding becomes completely natural. However, by limiting his strength to no more than 7 HCP with his initial response, responder has considerably more mobility in subsequent bidding. For example:

	(I)	OPENER	RESPONDER
		♠ A K Q 10	♠ 4 3 2
		♡ A K Q 10 7 2	♡ 8 6 5
		◊ A 3	◊ 5 4
		♣ 8	♣ 10 9 5 3 2

Precision bidding:

1♣	1◊
2♡¹	2NT²
3♠³	4♡⁴
Pass	

¹ Describes a strong two-bid; responder cannot pass.
² Respecting partner's force, responder makes the most discouraging bid possible. (Usually 0-3 HCP.)
³ Showing his second suit. Any new suit, after announcing a strong two-bid is 100% forcing in Precision, as it would be using standard methods.
⁴ In spite of his Yarborough, responder is forced to bid again.

	(J)	OPENER	RESPONDER
		♠ A K Q J 7 4 3	♠ 9 8 5
		♡ A Q	♡ 7 4 3
		◊ Q 5 4	◊ A J 10 9 7
		♣ A	♣ 8 6

Precision bidding:

1♣	1◊
2♠	3◊¹
3♠²	4♠³
6♠⁴	Pass

[1] Responder could support spades immediately, but since he is in the upper range for a negative response, he shows he has some values and a reasonable diamond suit prior to raising opener's suit.

[2] Encouraged to learn that partner is not completely broke and that he has a diamond suit worth bidding, opener elects to rebid his solid seven-card suit and await developments. Remember, opener does not have to fear that the bidding will die short of game, having shown a strong two-bid, with responder having indicated some values.

[3] Having shown his diamond suit and some strength (within the 0-7 point range), responder supports spades leaving the decision as to HOW HIGH up to partner.

[4] With partner having values in diamonds and even a mild fit for spades, prospects for slam are excellent. Bid what you think you can make!

Before turning our attention to the opener's rebids after a positive response, let us consider an illustration where the opener holds 4-4-4-1 distribution after a 1 ◊ response.

(K)	OPENER	RESPONDER
	♠ A K J 10	♠ 9 8 4
	♡ 5	♡ J 10 8 3 2
	◊ A Q 10 3	◊ K 4
	♣ K 10 8 6	♣ J 7 2

Precision bidding:

1 ♣	1 ◊
1 ♠ [1]	2 ♠ [2]
Pass [3]	

[1] Only choice of rebids with notrump out of the question and no five-card suit.

[2] Since partner has suggested a five-card suit, xxx is adequate support. Although 1 ♠ isn't forcing, responder wishes to show moderate values and mild interest in game if partner holds a maximum 1 ♠ bid.

[3] With a minimum and only four spades, opener declines partner's invitation to bid on. (Note that although 2 ♠ is not bullet-proof, it is certainly a playable contract even with only seven trump. As a matter of fact, it is probably the best contract on this deal outside of 1 ♠.)

Observe that with the sole exceptions of the Stayman Convention after a notrump rebid and 2NT to show a bust after a strong two-bid (both being inherent parts of standard bidding systems), all bidding after the 1 ♣ opening and the negative 1 ◊ response is both natural and straightforward. In addition to Precision's simplicity, you have the tremendous advantage of knowing immediately the limits of partner's high card strength. This information plus the Limited Bid Strategy should give you a good idea early in the auction whether you are in part score, game, or slam territory. With "How High" answered, you can turn your attention to "Where."

After a positive suit response

If you open with 1♣ and partner pleasantly surprises you by making a positive suit response (1♡, 1♠, 2♣, or 2♢), both of you know immediately that game is very likely since responder must have at least 8 HCP. As a general rule, you should consider a positive response forcing to game. The only exception is when both hands are minimum, an adequate trump suit cannot be found, and notrump is unplayable.

As with the negative 1♢ response, the opener should proceed by bidding naturally. Show a good five-card or longer suit of your own or raise partner's suit as strongly as your hand dictates. Holding a balanced hand, bid an appropriate number of notrump depending on the strength of your hand. Should you be blessed with a strong two-bid, after a positive response jump in your suit as you would after a 1♢ response (keeping in mind that now not only game but slam is a distinct possibility).

Except for opener's strong two-bid, there is rarely any reason to jump in subsequent bidding after a positive response. Remember, the partnership is virtually forced to game after the initial response. Consequently, jump rebids can be used to describe good two-suiters and solid suits. You never have to jump simply to keep the bidding open. Any simple change of suit is forcing and cannot be passed. As a matter of fact, any simple rebid of your suit at a low level is 100% forcing.

Let us consider a few examples:

(A)	OPENER	RESPONDER
	♠ A Q 10 2	♠ K 8 5
	♡ K 4	♡ A 10 9 5 3
	♢ K 10 5 3	♢ A Q J 7
	♣ A J 6	♣ K

Precision bidding:

1♣	1♡[1]
1NT[2]	2♢[3]
3♢[4]	4NT[5]
5♡[6]	5NT[7]
6♡[8]	7♢[9]
Pass	

¹ Regular positive suit response — 8 or more HCP and at least a five-card heart suit.

² Balanced, 16-18 point hand.

³ Although slam is almost certain, there is no need to jump the bidding at this point; 2 ◊ is 100% forcing. Keep the bidding low to give your side ample room for exploration. You may have a good idea regarding the answer to the question, "How High," but you need more information to determine the best "Where."

⁴ Promising four-card diamond support and, by inference, denying three-card heart support. With three hearts you would have chosen to raise hearts, knowing your side had an eight-card fit.

⁵ Having answered the question "Where," it is only a matter of aces and kings to determine "How High." The Blackwood Convention* will give the answer.

⁶ "2 aces."

⁷ "We have all the aces; how many kings do you have?"

⁸ "2 kings."

⁹ Since partner is known to have no worse than the king doubleton of hearts (he can't hold three or he would have raised hearts over 2 ◊), a discard is available on the ace of clubs for the potential spade loser, and the trump suit is solid with partner's known king. Therefore, 13 tricks should be available in diamonds.

(Isn't bridge an easy game? Well, at least it was on this Precise grand slam!)

(B)	OPENER	RESPONDER
	♠ A Q 5	♠ K J 10
	♡ 7 6	♡ Q 8 4 3 2
	◊ K Q J 4	◊ 5 3 2
	♣ K J 7 2	♣ Q 6

Precision bidding:

1 ♣	1 ♡¹
1NT²	2NT³
Pass⁴	

¹ 8 or more HCP and five or more hearts.

---

*4NT (once agreement on a trump suit has either been agreed or implied) asks how many aces partner holds. Partner bids: 5 ♣: 0-4; 5 ◊: 1; 5 ♡: 2; 5 ♠: 3. If the partnership holds all the aces, kings are asked for by bidding 5NT, which always shows that the side has all of the aces. Responses are the same at the six-level.

[2] Balanced 16-18 point hand. (Just like opening a strong NT.)

[3] Having already shown a five-card heart suit and 8 HCP, responder (using the Limited Bid Strategy) is not strong enough to force to game. Hence, he invites partner to continue on to game with anything above a minimum 1NT rebid.

[4] "Sorry partner, I also have minimum values and no fit for hearts."

(C)	OPENER	RESPONDER
	♠ A Q 7 6 4	♠ 8 2
	♡ 9 5	♡ K J 7 3 2
	◇ A 8 3	◇ Q J 6
	♣ A Q 5	♣ J 8 2

Precision bidding:

1 ♣	1 ♡
1 ♠[1]	1NT[2]
2NT[3]	Pass[4]

[1] Natural, suggesting a five-card suit.

[2] Minimum rebid; no second suit, scattered strength.

[3] Non-forcing, invitational raise showing a 16 point 1♣ opening and a fairly balanced hand without three-card heart support. (Responder knows opener holds only 16 HCP since with 17 or more opener would have insisted on game.)

[4] With an 8 point minimum and no fit in either hearts or spades, responder stops short of game.

Note that both (B) and (C) were examples where responder made a positive response and game contracts were not reached. In both cases opener and responder held absolute minimum values and no fit was found. Hopeless game contracts were avoided in both illustrations.

(D)	OPENER	RESPONDER
	♠ A 9 8	♠ K J 10 6 4 3
	♡ A 8 7 6	♡ 5
	◇ Q J 8	◇ K 10 4
	♣ A Q 9	♣ J 10 7

Precision bidding:

1 ♣	1 ♠
1NT[1]	2 ♠[2]
3 ♠[3]	4 ♠[4]
Pass

¹ Describing opener's balanced, strong notrump. Although Axx is adequate support to raise partner's known five-card suit, 1NT is a far better description of the 4-3-3-3 minimum 1 ♣ opener. Opener intends to raise spades later and responder cannot pass 1NT.
² Promising at least six spades since 1 ♠ guaranteed five.
³ Establishing the fit.
⁴ A good trump suit has been found after a 1 ♣ opening and positive response, so game must be reached. Responder has no interest in slam, so he properly brings the auction to an end.

(E)	OPENER	RESPONDER
	♠ J 8	♠ 9 7 4
	♡ A K J 8 4 2	♡ Q 10 3
	◊ 9 8	◊ A Q 10 5 4
	♣ A K 4	♣ 7 5

Precision bidding:

1 ♣	2 ◊¹
2 ♡²	3 ♡³
4 ♡⁴	Pass

¹ Positive suit response — 8 or more HCP and five or more diamonds.
² Five or more hearts; 16-21 HCP.
³ Heart support; three-card support is ample since partner has shown a five-card suit.
⁴ A good place to play game with no interest in slam.

(F)	OPENER	RESPONDER
	♠ K J	♠ Q 10 7 6 3
	♡ A Q 10 7	♡ K J 8 4
	◊ A Q 9 5	◊ K 8 3
	♣ K J 8	♣ 6

Precision bidding:

1 ♣	1 ♠
2NT¹	3 ♡²
4 ♡³	Pass⁴

¹ Balanced hand with 19-21 HCP. (The same bid opener would have made over a 1 ◊ response.)
² Hoping to find a major suit fit but willing to play 3NT if partner doesn't have three spades or four hearts.

[3] "I have four hearts."
[4] "Fine, I don't have the values for slam so the heart game should be our best contract."

(G)	OPENER	RESPONDER
	♠ A K Q J 8 5	♠ 10 9 4
	♡ A K 8	♡ Q 7
	◊ K 3	◊ A Q 9 5 4
	♣ K 8	♣ 7 6 3

Precision bidding:

1♣	2◊
3♠[1]	4♠[2]
4NT[3]	5◊[4]
6♠[5]	Pass

[1] Showing a strong two-bid in spades. Although 2♠ would be 100% forcing, opener jumps to inform partner of his exceptional strength and solid suit. (Alerting partner immediately to the excellent slam prospects.)
[2] With an absolute minimum positive response and support for partner's suit, responder simply raises leaving the next move up to the opener.
[3] "How many aces, partner?"
[4] "One."
[5] "One minor suit ace should be our only loser since I have the other suit protected from two quick losers by my Kx."

Finally, let us consider the 1♣ opener's rebid when he holds 4-4-4-1 distribution with his singleton in responder's suit. Obviously, opener has a convenient raise of partner's suit if his singleton is elsewhere.

(H)	OPENER	RESPONDER
	♠ 4	♠ K Q J 9 2
	♡ A Q J 7	♡ K 10 5 3
	◊ J 10 8 6	◊ 7 3
	♣ A K J 3	♣ 8 6

Precision bidding:

1♣	1♠
1NT[1]	2♡[2]
3♡[3]	4♡[4]
Pass	

[1] Least of evils. Although you would usually have a balanced or semi-balanced hand for this rebid, 1NT is preferable to freely bidding a suit at the two-level which partner must assume is five cards in length. You have denied holding a good five-card suit (which is true) and you simply will have to owe partner a spade!

[2] Exploring further for a possible major suit fit.

[3] "I have four-card heart support. Do you have anything else of interest?"

[4] "No, let's stop at game."

After a positive notrump response

If you open 1 ♣ and partner makes a positive notrump response (1NT: 8-10; 2NT: 11-13; or 3NT: 14-15 HCP), you should act just as though he had opened the bidding with a very weak or intermediate notrump bid. Thus, if you have one or two four-card majors, you should use the Stayman Convention (by bidding clubs as cheaply as possible) in order to search for a 4-4 major suit fit. Alternatively, you can bid a long suit of your own (which is forcing), jump in a suit to describe a strong two-bid, or raise notrump appropriately.

A notrump response places the opening 1 ♣ bidder in an excellent position to make full use of the Limited Bid Strategy. He knows responder's point count and that partner holds a balanced hand without any singletons or five-card suits. It is usually a simple matter for the opener to set the final contract. He often can do this with a single bid.

Here are a few examples:

(A)	OPENER	RESPONDER
	♠ K Q 10 3	♠ A J 7 2
	♡ A J 10	♡ K 6
	◇ A K J 7	◇ 10 9 6 4
	♣ 8 5	♣ J 10 3

Precision bidding:

1 ♣	1NT[1]
2 ♣[2]	2 ♠[3]
4 ♠[4]	Pass

[1] 8-10 HCP and a balanced hand.

[2] Although opener knows the partnership has the assets for 3NT, 4 ♠ is

likely to be a superior contract if responder has a four-card spade suit. The Stayman Convention will locate a 4-4 fit if one exists.

³ "I have four spades."

⁴ Using the Limited Bid Strategy, opener can tell that game should be bid but slam is out of reach — so he concludes the auction by bidding the spade game.

(Note that 3NT could easily fail, despite two balanced hands, whereas 4♠ is almost certain to make.)

(B)	OPENER	RESPONDER
	♠ A 4 2	♠ K J
	♡ K Q J 9 6	♡ 10 8 3
	◇ J	◇ Q 8 3 2
	♣ A J 9 3	♣ K 7 5 4

Precision bidding:

1♣	1NT
2♡¹	3♡²
4♡³	Pass

¹ Natural and obviously forcing; promising at least a five-card suit.

² Heart support — three-card support is adequate when partner has shown at least five.

³ With no interest in slam, opener simply carries on to game.

(C)	OPENER	RESPONDER
	♠ Q 10 9 6	♠ K J 7
	♡ A K J 10	♡ 9 4
	◇ A J	◇ Q 10 5 2
	♣ J 10 3	♣ A 9 5 4

Precision bidding:

1♣	1NT
2♣¹	2◇²
2NT³	3NT⁴
Pass	

¹ The Stayman Convention.

² No four-card major.

³ Since opener holds a minimum 16 HCP he cannot force to game in case

responder also holds a minimum. Hence, he only invites game by re-bidding 2NT, knowing partner does not hold four cards in either major.

[4] With a maximum 1NT response responder cheerfully carries on to game knowing the partnership must have at least 26 HCP.

(D)	OPENER	RESPONDER
	♠ K Q 7	♠ A 9 3
	♡ Q J 10	♡ K 5 2
	◊ A Q 4	◊ 9 8 5 2
	♣ Q 4 3 2	♣ J 8 6

Precision bidding:

1♣	1NT
2NT[1]	Pass[2]

[1] With a minimum 16-count and no interest in the majors, game in no-trump is the only hope. However, opener cannot force to game since the partnership may have only 24 HCP — just short of the strength required for game in notrump. Hence, he invites responder to carry on with anything above a minimum 1NT response.

[2] Holding absolute minimum values responder is forced to decline partner's game-try and pass.

(E)	OPENER	RESPONDER
	♠ K Q J 8 6 3	♠ 10 9
	♡ A	♡ Q 10 7 4
	◊ K Q 10 2	◊ A 7 5
	♣ J 10	♣ Q 9 4 3

Precision bidding:

1♣	1NT
4♠[1]	Pass[2]

[1] Opener knows that responder has at least two spades giving the partnership an eight-card fit (minimum). With enough playing strength for game (slam being out of reach), opener concludes the auction by bidding the spade game.

[2] Respecting partner's sign-off. (Even if responder held a maximum 1NT response he would be obligated to pass since the opener has no interest beyond game.)

(F)   OPENER

    ♠ Q 10 7 5

    ♡ A K 10 3

    ◊ A Q

    ♣ J 8 7

                         RESPONDER

                         ♠ A K J 9

                         ♡ J 4 2

                         ◊ K 10 8 5

                         ♣ 10 3

Precision bidding:

1 ♣	2NT[1]
3 ♣[2]	3 ♠[3]
4 ♠[4]	Pass

[1] 11-13 HCP and a balanced hand.

[2] The Stayman Convention (not a club suit) attempting to locate a 4-4 major suit fit.

[3] "I have four spades."

[4] "Fine. We don't have the values for slam but 4 ♠ should be our best game contract."

(G)   OPENER

    ♠ A Q

    ♡ A Q J

    ◊ K Q J 7

    ♣ Q 10 9 4

                          RESPONDER

                         ♠ K 10 6 3

                         ♡ K 8 7 2

                         ◊ 10 9

                         ♣ A K 5

Precision bidding:

1 ♣	2NT
4NT[1]	6NT[2]
Pass	

[1] Quantitative raise using the Limited Bid Strategy. Opener holds 21 HCP opposite 11-13 HCP. If responder has more than a minimum 2NT response a small slam in notrump should be a reasonable undertaking. Even if partner has minimum values and passes 4NT, it should not be a disaster on this deal with the partnership holding at least 32 HCP in the combined hands.

[2] Holding a maximum 2NT response, responder accepts partner's invitation and bids the small slam in notrump.

(Remember, 4NT in this auction should not be confused with the Blackwood Convention — 4NT: asking for aces. If opener wanted to ask for aces he would have bid 4 ♣ — the Gerber Convention. *)

---

*Responder bids: 4 ◊, 0 or 4; 4 ♡, 1; 4 ♠, 2; 4NT, 3; 5 ♣ by opener then asks for kings with the same responses one level higher.

After an unusual positive response

If you open 1 ♣ and partner makes an Unusual Positive response (2 ♡, 2 ♠, 3 ♣, or 3 ◊), you know his exact distribution — 4-4-4-1 with the singleton in the suit he bid. You also know he has a minimum of eight high card points, making game almost certain.

Your first obligation after an Unusual Positive response is to set the trump suit, or warn partner that no good trump suit exists by bidding no-trump with his singleton suit well-stopped. If you do name a trump suit and responder has extra values (beyond the 8-10 point minimum range), he can begin slam investigation at a relatively low level by simply bidding a new suit which suggests a feature in the new suit bid. (In technical bridge terms this is referred to as "cue-bidding," because responder is not suggesting the new suit as trump since you've already established the trump suit.) If responder holds a minimum Unusual Positive, he can simply raise the suit you've set as trump.

Let's consider a few examples:

	(A)	OPENER	RESPONDER
		♠ A K 9 8 4	♠ J
		♡ 10 9	♡ Q 8 7 3
		◊ K Q 10	◊ A J 9 4
		♣ A Q 5	♣ J 10 7 4

Precision bidding:

1 ♣	2 ♠[1]
2NT[2]	3NT[3]
Pass	

[1] 1-4-4-4 distribution with a singleton spade. 8 or more HCP.
[2] Opener holds sufficient spade strength to play notrump in spite of responder's singleton. He also knows there is no good trump suit available and must inform partner of this fact immediately.
[3] Being in the lower range (8-10 HCP), responder settles for the no-trump game since no good trump suit exists.

	(B)	OPENER	RESPONDER
		♠ A 10 7	♠ K 9 8 4
		♡ K J	♡ A Q 10 6
		◊ K J 10 8 6	◊ Q 9 7 4
		♣ A 7 5	♣ 3

Precision bidding:

1♣	3♣
3◇[1]	3♡[2]
3♠[3]	4♠[4]
4NT[5]	5◇[6]
6◇[7]	Pass

[1] Setting the trump suit; opener has a very good hand in light of partner's response despite holding a 16-point minimum 1♣ opener. There is no wastage in the club suit (the ace covers partner's known singleton), and the partnership has a fine 5-4 diamond fit.

[2] Having more than a minimum Unusual Positive, responder shows his heart feature. (Remember, it is agreed that diamonds is the trump suit.)

[3] "Glad to hear you have more than a minimum Unusual Positive; I have a spade feature."

[4] "I have a spade feature also."

[5] "How many aces do you have?"

[6] "One."

[7] "O.K., we are off an ace but we should have an excellent play for 12 tricks with diamonds as trump."

(When this deal was played at a recent national bridge tournament several pairs reached a hopeless 3NT contract after a strong 1NT opening and subsequent Stayman auction. After dislodging the ace, their opponents won four club tricks in addition to the ◇A. The 6◇ contract, reached after a simple Precision auction, was virtually unbreakable.'

Although it comes up less often than the other responses, when it does the Unusual Positive is one of the most devastating weapons in your Precision arsenal. It frequently leads to bidding excellent slams with considerably less than the usual 33 points, and avoids getting too high when the partnership has a lot of High Card Points but no good fit.

We have now covered all the responses and rebids after a 1♣ opening bid. As you can see, it is really rather straightforward after both partners have limited their strength. With the exception of a few useful tools (such as Stayman, Blackwood, and the "cue-bid" after an Unusual Positive response), everything is completely natural. After a 1♣ opening, you and your partner should have little or no trouble answering our two questions: WHERE? HOW HIGH? In short, you should be able to "CLUB" your opponents to death.

Before we move on to notrump openings, let's find out how well you understand the 1♣ opening, initial responses, and rebids.

Exercise #1
1 ♣ openings, responses, and rebids

What initial action would you take as the dealer with the following hands?

1. ♠ A Q J 10 9 8
♡ A K Q 10
◇ A K
♣ 4

2. ♠ K Q 10
♡ A Q 9 2
◇ K Q J 4
♣ A Q

3. ♠ A Q 5 2
♡ K Q J 10 6
◇ K J 9 2
♣ –

4. ♠ Q J
♡ K Q J
◇ K Q J
♣ J 10 7 3 2

Partner opens 1 ♣; what initial response would you make with the following hands?

5. ♠ Q J 10 9 3 2
♡ K 8 7 4
◇ 6
♣ 10 9

6. ♠ A 10 5 2
♡ K 6 5
◇ Q J 10 8 3
♣ 4

7. ♠ A Q 10
♡ J 10 3
◇ K J 10 2
♣ 9 8 2

8. ♠ J 10 6 3 2
♡ A K Q J
◇ 7 4
♣ 8 6

9. ♠ 9 7
♡ K Q J 10
◇ K 10 2
♣ 9 8 4 2

10. ♠ A Q J 10
♡ 7
◇ 10 9 8 2
♣ 10 9 8 2

11. ♠ A Q
♡ K Q 9 6
◇ Q J 10 2
♣ J 10 3

12. ♠ A Q 7
♡ K 10
◇ 9 7 6 3 2
♣ J 10 5

13. ♠ 10 9 7 3 2
♡ A K 4
◇ 7 5
♣ K 3 2

14. ♠ J 10 4 3 2
♡ A 7
◇ A Q J 10 4
♣ 4

15. ♠ A K Q 10 7 2
♡ A J 10
◇ 5
♣ K 9 8

16. ♠ A K 10
♡ K J 10 3
◇ Q 10 2
♣ K J 4

Partner responds 1 ◇ to your 1 ♣ opening; what is your next bid holding:

17. ♠ K Q 7
♡ A Q
◇ K 10 8 3
♣ A Q 7 6

18. ♠ A Q 10 9 2
♡ K Q J 10
◇ A J 7
♣ Q

19. ♠ A K Q 10 9 4 3
♡ A K Q 10
◇ K 6
♣ –

20. ♠ A 10 9 2
    ♡ K Q J 5
    ◊ 5
    ♣ A Q 10 2

21. ♠ K J 10 2
    ♡ A Q J 7
    ◊ Q 10 3
    ♣ K J

22. ♠ J 10 4 3 2
    ♡ A Q
    ◊ A Q 10
    ♣ K J 2

23. ♠ A Q J 10
    ♡ A 8 2
    ◊ 7
    ♣ A J 10 9 4

OPENER	RESPONDER
1♣	1◊
1♡	?

24. ♠ K 10 9 2
    ♡ J 8 7 3
    ◊ 8 7 4
    ♣ K 3

25. ♠ Q 10 3
    ♡ 9 7
    ◊ Q 10 5 2
    ♣ Q J 9 4

26. ♠ 8 7 4 3
    ♡ 7 6 2
    ◊ J 10 6 3
    ♣ 8 3

OPENER	RESPONDER
1♣	1◊
1NT	?

27. ♠ Q 10 9 2
    ♡ K J 10 4
    ◊ J 10 2
    ♣ 9 8

28. ♠ 5
    ♡ J 10 9 5 3 2
    ◊ 8 7 4 2
    ♣ 5 3

OPENER	RESPONDER
1♣	1◊
2♡	?

29. ♠ 7 5 3 2
    ♡ 9 7
    ◊ J 10 5 3 2
    ♣ J 3

30. ♠ K 10 9
    ♡ 9 8
    ◊ K 10 5 2
    ♣ J 10 7 6

OPENER	RESPONDER
1♣	1◊
2NT	?

31. ♠ J 10 9 4
    ♡ Q 10 9 3
    ◊ K 4
    ♣ 8 7 3

32. ♠ Q J 9 7 6 4
    ♡ 5 3 2
    ◊ 9 8 5
    ♣ 4

33. ♠ 4
    ♡ K J 10 7 6 3
    ◊ Q 10 4
    ♣ 7 6 3

OPENER	RESPONDER
1♣	1♡
?	

34. ♠ A 10 9 2
♡ Q 10 6
◇ A K 8 7
♣ K J

35. ♠ A Q 10
♡ J 7
◇ A K J 3
♣ A J 9 8

OPENER	RESPONDER
1♣	1♠
?	

36. ♠ K 10 6 5
♡ A K J 6
◇ A Q J
♣ 5 2

37. ♠ Q 8 7 4
♡ A K Q
◇ A J 10 2
♣ K Q

OPENER	RESPONDER
1♣	1♠
1NT	?

38. ♠ K 10 9 4 2
♡ A J 7
◇ Q 10 4
♣ 9 8

39. ♠ K J 10 9 7 4
♡ 6
◇ A J 3
♣ 10 9 5

40. ♠ A Q 10 6 3
♡ A 7 6
◇ K J 10 9 2
♣ –

OPENER	RESPONDER
1♣	1♡
2♣	?

41. ♠ K 10 4 3
♡ A J 10 5 2
◇ 9 8 4
♣ 7

42. ♠ 4 2
♡ A Q J 3 2
◇ 9 8 4
♣ Q 8 3

OPENER	RESPONDER
1♣	1NT
?	

43. ♠ K Q 10 2
♡ 8 7
◇ A K J 3
♣ K J 6

44. ♠ K Q J
♡ A Q J 10 8 3
◇ K J 10
♣ 5

	OPENER	RESPONDER
	1♣	2NT
	?	

45. ♠ K J 10 9 3   **46.** ♠ A K
  ♡ A 10   ♡ J 10 9 7 4 3
  ◇ K Q 6   ◇ A Q J 7
  ♣ K 4 3   ♣ J

	OPENER	RESPONDER
	1♣	2◇
	2♡	?

47. ♠ J 10 5 2   **48.** ♠ 5
  ♡ 8 6   ♡ J 6
  ◇ A K J 7 3   ◇ A Q J 10 3
  ♣ 5 2   ♣ K Q J 10 7

	OPENER	RESPONDER
	1♣	2♡
	?	

49. ♠ 9 8 4 2   **50.** ♠ J 10 3
  ♡ A 9 4 2   ♡ A K J 10 4
  ◇ A K Q   ◇ K Q
  ♣ K 7   ♣ K J 7

	OPENER	RESPONDER
	1♣	3♣
	3♡	?

51. ♠ A Q 8 3   **52.** ♠ Q 10 7 6
  ♡ K 10 9 3   ♡ K 8 3 2
  ◇ A 5 3 2   ◇ K J 10 4
  ♣ 7   ♣ 9

	OPENER	RESPONDER
	1♣	3NT
	?	

53. ♠ A Q 10 3   **54.** ♠ A 5
  ♡ K J 10 7   ♡ Q J 9 6 4 3
  ◇ A Q 8 5   ◇ K Q J
  ♣ J   ♣ Q J

Answers
Exercise #1

1. 1♣
There is no upper limit to the strength of a Precision 1♣ opening. It is your only forcing bid. A jump shift in spades after partner's initial response will describe your strong Standard American two-bid.

2. 2NT
The only exception to opening 1♣ when you hold more than 15 HCP is the 2NT opening which describes a balanced 22-24 HCP.

3. 1♣
Opening 1♣ does not promise any length or strength in clubs. It simply says you have a good hand with at least 16 HCP.

4. 1♣
Although it is hard to imagine a worse 16 count, despite the poor quality of your points you still do have 16 of them. Hence, you must open 1♣.

5. 1◇
You cannot bid your fine spade suit directly, since you lack the required 8 HCP for a positive response. Respond 1◇ alerting partner to your limited high card strength; then show your fine spade suit.

6. 2◇
You cannot bid 1◇ since that would be a negative response showing 0-7 HCP, saying nothing about diamonds.

7. 2NT
Describing your balanced 11-13 HCP with scattered strength.

8. 1♠
You cannot make a positive suit response in a four-card suit. Therefore, you must respond 1♠ showing your five-card spade suit (and at least 8 HCP), intending to show your powerful heart suit during the next round of bidding.

9. 1NT
Describing your balanced 8-10 HCP without a five-card major or good five-card minor.

10. 2♡
The Unusual Positive response showing 8 or more HCP, specifically 4-4-4-1 distribution, and a singleton in the suit bid.

11. 3NT
Describing your balanced 14-15 HCP without a five-card major or good five-card minor.

12. 1NT
With such a weak five-card minor it is best to consider your hand balanced and respond 1NT showing 8-10 HCP.

13. 1♠
Although you may choose not to make a positive suit response in a weak five-card minor suit, you must *never* by-pass a five-card major.

14. 1♠
With two five-card suits and the values for a positive response, you should always respond in the higher ranking suit first, irrespective of their relative strength.

15. 1♠
There is no other appropriate response with this powerhouse. A small slam is almost certain and prospects for a grand slam are excellent. Nonetheless, your only possible response is a game-forcing 1♠. You'll reveal your exceptional strength later in the auction.

16. 2NT
When responder is blessed with more than 15 HCP and a balanced hand, he should respond 2NT and then drive the bidding toward slam subsequently.

17. 2NT
Describing 19-21 HCP and a balanced hand.

18. 1♠
Promising a five-card suit (unless opener is specifically 4-1-4-4) and 16-21 HCP. Not forcing.

19. 2♠
Showing a strong two-bid in spades. Responder is forced to game.

20. 1♡
One of the rare cases where opener is

forced to introduce a four-card suit after a negative 1 ◊ response.

21. 1NT
Opener is showing a standard strong (16-18) notrump opening.

22. 1♠
Opener should never by-pass a five-card major, even with a relatively weak suit and a fairly balanced hand with scattered strength.

23. 2♣
Do not be influenced by your fine four-card spade suit. Should partner bid over 2♣, you will be happy to introduce your spade suit in the auction, promising no more than a four-card suit.

24. 3♡
You have a maximum 1 ◊ response and excellent support for hearts. Jump to 3♡ inviting opener to carry on to game with anything above a minimum 1♣ opener.

25. 1NT
Having already limited the hand to no more than 7 HCP, you can now rebid 1NT describing your scattered 7 count lacking a fit for partner's heart suit. Remember, opener may have rebid 1♡ with 20 or 21 points, just short of a strong two-bid.

26. Pass
Even if partner has a maximum 1♡ rebid, game is out of the question. 1♡ is not forcing, so pass and hope he can make it.

27. 2♣
The Stayman Convention asking opener to bid a four-card major. Should partner bid 2 ◊ over 2♣, invite partner to go on to game by bidding 2NT.

28. 2♡
A sign-off simply informing partner that you have no interest in game and 2♡ will play better than 1NT. Your hand probably won't take a trick in notrump, but it should produce a few tricks in hearts.

29. 2NT
Respecting partner's forcing rebid, responder makes the most discouraging rebid possible (0-3 HCP).

30. 3NT
Since responder cannot bid 2NT which

would describe a bust, he jumps in notrump to show his balanced maximum 1 ◊ response.

31. 3♣
The Stayman Convention. Exploring for a possible major suit fit. If no fit is found, responder intends to sign-off in 3NT.

32. 3♠
Bidding 3♠ over a 2NT rebid by opener is similar to bidding 2♠ over a 1NT rebid. It is a sign-off simply saying that 3♠ will play better than 2NT. Opener is expected to pass unless he has an absolute maximum with an excellent fit for spades and wishes to take a chance, e.g., ♠K1053 ♡AK76 ◊AK3 ♣A6.

33. 4♡
Partner's 2NT rebid promises at least two hearts, giving your side at least an eight-card fit as well as sufficient strength for game. Since 3♡ would be a sign-off, you must jump to 4♡ with game-going values.

34. 2♡
Establish your known eight-card major suit fit immediately. A simple raise promises 16-18 HCP and three-card support which is exactly what you have.

35. 2NT
Describing your balanced 19-21 point hand.

36. 3♠
Describing 19-20 HCP and excellent support for responder's suit.

37. 4♠
Describing 21-22 HCP and excellent support for responder's suit. This is by no means a sign-off. In light of responder's positive response, slam is possible if responder holds more than a minimum positive.

38. 3NT
Having already shown a five-card spade suit, responder should proceed directly to 3NT knowing the partnership has between 26 and 28 HCP.

39. 4♠
Partner has shown a strong (16-18) notrump which means your side has both the values for game and an eight-card spade fit. Jump directly to game.

40. 3 ◊

Jump shift to show your powerful 5-5 distribution and slam interest. Since 2 ◊ would be 100% forcing (after your initial positive response), 3 ◊ promises at least 5-5.

41. 2 ♠

Describe your hand by bidding your second suit. 2 ♠ does not promise additional values as it would in standard bidding methods.

42. 3 ♣

No reason to repeat hearts since 1 ♡ already promised a five-card suit. Show your support for partner's suit.

43. 2 ♣

You have ample strength to raise directly to 3NT, but you should first explore for a possible 4-4- major suit fit in spades. 2 ♣ is the Stayman Convention asking partner to bid a four-card major.

44. 4 ♡

Your side has both the values for game and an eight-card heart fit. Remember, whenever you can answer both questions (WHERE and HOW HIGH), set the final contract.

45. 3 ♠

Obviously forcing and asking responder to raise spades with three or four and bid 3NT with a doubleton.

46. 4 ♡

Setting the final contract. Opener knows the partnership has at least eight hearts and slam is out of the question, even if responder holds a maximum 2NT response.

47. 2 ♠

Showing your second suit.

48. 4 ♣

Jump to 4 ♣ to describe your fine hand and 5-5 distribution. Since 3 ♣ would be 100% forcing, 4 ♣ must show 5-5 or better in your two suits and some slam interest.

49. 2 ♠

Opener's first obligation over the Unusual Positive response is to suggest a good trump suit. Your side has a four-four spade fit which should be established immediately.

50. 3NT

Inform responder immediately that no suit fit exists and that you have both game-going values and hearts well-protected. With a minimum 16 count you should only bid 2NT, since you cannot be sure there is game unless partner holds more than the eight-point minimum.

51. 3 ♠

You have far more than a minimum Unusual Positive response. Partner has suggested a good trump fit exists in hearts, so inform partner of your extra values by cue-bidding your spades.

52. 4 ♡

You have a minimum Unusual Positive response and should do no more than raise hearts to game.

53. 4 ♣

The Stayman Convention asking partner to bid a four-card major.

54. 4 ♡

Sign-off in the major suit game with your absolute minimum 1 ♣ opener. 4 ♡ should play far better than 3NT with your six-card suit.

Chapter 4

Precision Notrump Bidding

BALANCED MINIMUM (13-15 HCP) opening bids cause no end of difficulty for players using standard bidding methods. Thousands of pages have been written to explain the right order in which to bid your suits, and how strong a suit must be in order to bid it. Even if you manage to digest and learn all this, your problems are far from over! Since your opening bid of one of a suit in standard methods is nearly unlimited, opposite a balanced minimum opening, partner may get unduly excited with a minimum hand and push the bidding to disastrous heights.

Precision handles these troublemaking hands effectively and simply. The most important vehicle for accomplishing this is the intermediate 1NT opening, which — with the aid of the Limited Bid Strategy — you'll find as easy to use as the standard notrump range you no doubt presently play.

The intermediate 1NT opening

The Precision 1NT opening shows 13-15 HCP and balanced distribution (4-3-3-3, 4-4-3-2, or 5-3-3-2 with a relatively weak five-card minor). Playing Precision you should open 1NT with any of the following hands:

(a) ♠ A Q 10 7   ♡ K Q 3   ◊ J 10 8 6   ♣ K 9

(b) ♠ J 10 4   ♡ A J 8   ◊ A Q   ♣ Q 5 4 3 2

(c) ♠ J 10 7 5   ♡ K Q 10 3   ◊ 7 4 2   ♣ A K

(d) ♠ 8 6   ♡ A J 10 3   ◊ K J 10 2   ♣ K J 3

You should not open the bidding 1NT when you have a five-card major suit. Needless to say, when you hold a six-card suit (either minor or major) the hand doesn't qualify as a 1NT opening. Consquently, the following hands should NOT be opened 1NT:

(e) ♠ J 5 4 3 2   ♡ A Q   ◊ K Q 10   ♣ Q J 9

Open 1 ♠, not 1NT. Even though your major suit is extremely weak, it is your most convenient opportunity to inform partner that you hold five spades. If you open 1NT partner will never know.

(f) ♠ A Q   ♡ K 10 7   ◊ J 10 6 4 3 2   ♣ K J

Despite the weakness of your six-card suit and your stoppers in all suits, it is best to open 1 ◊, not 1NT.

(g) ♠ Q J   ♡ K Q J 6   ◊ A 10 8   ♣ K 5 4 2

You can't open 1NT with this balanced hand, you have 16 HCP! Open 1 ♣.

Responding to 1NT

The strategy for responding to the Precision 1NT opening is exactly the same as in standard bidding. Except you must keep in mind that partner has shown a slightly weaker hand than in standard methods. Thus, if your partner opens 1NT, you first use the Limited Bid Strategy to determine your chances for game or slam. Then, you select your response from the following choices, depending on the combined partnership assets:

Game is out of reach: (You hold 0-9 HCP)
   1.   Sign-off by bidding 2 diamonds, 2 hearts, or 2 spades with a five card or longer suit.
   2.   Pass.

Game is possible: (You hold 10-11 HCP)
   1. Use the Stayman (2 ♣) Convention and make a minimum bid at your next turn. For example:

OPENER	RESPONDER	or	OPENER	RESPONDER
1NT	2 ♣		1NT	2 ♣
2 ♡	3 ♡		2 ♠	2NT
	Invitational			Invitational

   2. Raise to 2NT (balanced hand, no four-card or longer major suit).

Game (at least) should be bid: (You hold 12 HCP or more)

1. Use the Stayman (2 ♣) Convention and make a forcing or game-level bid at your next turn. For example:

OPENER	RESPONDER	or	OPENER	RESPONDER
1NT	2 ♣		1NT	2 ♣
2 ◊	3 ♡		2 ♠	4 ♠
	Forcing			

2. Raise to 3NT (balanced hand, no four-card or longer major suit).

3. Jump in a good five-card or longer suit. (Jumps to 3 ♣ and 3 ◊ deny a four-card major, since with a four-card major you would have used the Stayman Convention.)

4. Jump to game in a suit (4 ♡, 4 ♠, 5 ♣, 5 ◊).

(Although these methods are very practical and we recommend them for most partnerships, if you and your partner have more sophisticated machinery that works for you, by all means continue using it. Any approach that can be used over a standard strong notrump (or a weak notrump) can be adapted to the Precision intermediate 1NT opening, as long as you keep in mind opener's reduced high card range of 13-15 HCP. Simply adjust the point count ranges in using the Limited Bid Strategy.)

Let's see how these methods work. You partner opens 1NT in each of the following problems; what call do you make?

(a) ♠ 9 8 6 5 3 2   ♡ 6   ◊ J 10 6 4   ♣ 8 6

At notrump, your pitiful collection may not produce a trick for partner but is likely to take several tricks with spades as trump. Tactically, 2 ♠ may avoid the penalty double that 1NT was likely to receive. Bid 2 ♠ and hope for a better hand next deal — but by all means don't frown or whimper 2 ♠, revealing to your opponents the dire weakness of your hand.

(b) ♠ K J 10 4   ♡ A Q 10 5 3   ◊ K 3   ♣ J 5

Bid 2 ♣. You have the required strength for game either in a major suit or 3NT. Should partner respond either 2 ♡ or 2 ♠ you will simply raise to game. If partner responds 2 ◊, you should make a forcing jump to 3 ♡, asking partner to raise to 4 ♡ if he holds three-card support or bid 3NT with a doubleton heart.

(c) ♠ K 10 7   ♡ A Q 10 5 3   ◊ Q 10 6   ♣ K 3

Bid 3 ♡. Since you have the values for game and the choice of games is between 4 ♡ and 3NT, an immediate forcing jump to 3 ♡ will enable partner to set the final contract. If opener holds three or four hearts, he will raise to 4 ♡; if he only holds a doubleton heart, he will bid 3NT.

(d) ♠ J 10 4   ♡ 8 7   ◇ K Q 10 2   ♣ A 10 9 5

Raise to 2NT. Invitational, but non-forcing. If partner holds a maximum 1NT opening, your side should reach game according to the Limited Bid Strategy. If he holds less, your good 10 count (plus three tens) should provide adequate values for a final contract of 2NT.

(e) ♠ K Q 10 6 4 3   ♡ A J 6   ◇ Q 10 4   ♣ 8

Bid 4 ♠. You have the required strength and at least an eight-card major suit fit (your six plus partner's known minimum of two). Bid what you think you can make.

(f) ♠ K Q 7   ♡ A 3   ◇ A Q J 6   ♣ K 9 8 2

Bid 4NT. Quantitative raise asking partner to bid 6NT if he holds a maximum, pass 4NT with a minimum. If you wanted to ask for aces, you would bid 4 ♣, the Gerber Convention. (See pg. 43.)

Opening 2NT

In Precision an opening 2NT bid describes a balanced 22-24 point hand as it does in standard Goren methods. Consequently, you can use the methods you presently use. For partnerships without a clearly defined structure of responses, we advise the following:

Responding to a 2NT Opening Bid		
BID:	**MEANING:**	**HCP:**
3 ♣	The Stayman Convention	4-up
3 ◇, 3 ♡, 3 ♠	Five-card or longer suit; forcing to game. May be the start of a slam investigation.	4-up
3NT	Sign-off; no interest in the major suits.	4-8

4♣	The Gerber Convention (asking for aces). A subsequent bid of 5♣ asks for kings, promising all the aces.	Depends on Playing Strength
4♡, 4♠	Sign-off with a six-card or longer suit. No interest in slam.	3-8
4NT	Quantitative raise asking opener to pass with a minimum 2NT opener, bid 6NT with a maximum, or leave the decision up to responder by raising to 5NT with a good 23 point hand.	9-10
5♣, 5♢	Sign-off with a weak hand unsuited for 3NT, usually a seven-card broken suit.	4-8
5NT	Grand Slam TRY. Forces opener to bid at least 6NT and invites partner to bid 7NT with a maximum 2NT opener.	13-14
6NT	Sign-off.	11-12
7NT	Sign-off.	15-up

As with the 1NT opening, do not open 2NT when you hold a five-card major. It has been our experience that you will fare best by opening 1♣ when you hold a five-card major and then make a forcing rebid in that suit. Remember, you can never show a five-card major suit once you have responded or rebid in notrump after a 1♣ opener. Partner will never know you hold five cards in either hearts or spades. Frequently this will lead to reaching and failing in 3NT when four of a major would have been iron-clad.

Precision's notrump steps

One of the advantages of the Precision notrump structure is that it gives you the ability to open intermediate balanced hands with 1NT without giving up the strong 1NT opening bid. With the balanced hands of 16-18 high-card ponts, we simply open 1♣ and rebid 1NT. Precision also takes care of the balanced hands that are too strong for a standard 1NT opening but do not quite meet the requirements for either a demand two-bid or a strong 2NT opening. With these 19 to 21 point hands you simply open 1♣ and rebid 2NT. No fear that partner will pass your initial bid before you are able to reveal the true strength of your hand, as is often the case in standard bidding.

This structure also permits you to open balanced hands somewhat lighter than is usually safe playing standard methods. Rebidding 1NT after a 1 ◊ opening cannot show a balanced 13 to 15 point hand since you would have opened 1NT. Hence, rebidding 1NT after a 1 ◊ opening must be limited to an exceptional 11 point hand or a respectable 12 count. The ability to strike the first blow in the auction frequently gives your side a decided advantage, particularly if the auction becomes highly competitive. In the words of *Anon.*, the most prolific of all writers,

> "Twice armed is he who knows his cause is just,
> But thrice armed is he who gets his blow in fust!"

The following table outlines Precision's comprehensive structure of opening bids with balanced hands:

High Card Points:	Bid:
11-12	Open 1 ◊; rebid 1NT
13-15	Open 1NT
16-18	Open 1♣; rebid 1NT
19-21	Open 1♣; rebid 2NT
22-24	Open 2NT
25-27	Open 1♣; rebid 3NT
28-up	Open 1♣; follow with a forcing rebid

Let us review the methods we have been discussing.

Exercise #2
Notrump openings, responses and rebids

What initial action would you take as the dealer with the following hands?

1. ♠ 8 6 5 3 2 ♡ A Q ◊ K J 10 ♣ K J 10	**2.** ♠ Q J ♡ A Q 10 ◊ Q 6 5 3 2 ♣ K J 4	**3.** ♠ K Q J ♡ Q J ◊ Q J 10 5 ♣ K J 3 2
4. ♠ A Q 10 ♡ A K J 7 ◊ K Q 3 ♣ Q 5 4	**5.** ♠ A Q ♡ K J 10 ◊ J 10 7 6 4 3 ♣ K 10	**6.** ♠ K Q J ♡ A Q J 10 ◊ K Q ♣ A 10 9 4

7. ♠ A K Q J
   ♡ J 10 3 2
   ◊ J 10
   ♣ Q J 9

Partner opens 1NT; what initial response would you make with the following hands?

8. ♠ K J 10 5
   ♡ A 10 3 2
   ◊ K 7
   ♣ Q 10 4

9. ♠ J 10 4
   ♡ Q 6
   ◊ A 10 9 6 2
   ♣ A 9 5

10. ♠ A Q J 10 5
    ♡ J 10 4
    ◊ K 6
    ♣ K 7 6

11. ♠ K Q 10 7 6 4
    ♡ A J
    ◊ Q J 10 9
    ♣ 3

12. ♠ Q 8 7 6 3 2
    ♡ 5
    ◊ 10 9 7 4
    ♣ 7 3

13. ♠ K Q 10
    ♡ A Q
    ◊ K Q 10 7
    ♣ K 10 7 6

14. ♠ 7
    ♡ K 4
    ◊ A K J 10 7 4
    ♣ K 9 8 3

15. ♠ A K 10
    ♡ K Q 10
    ◊ A J 5 3
    ♣ K 8 5

16. ♠ 5 3
    ♡ 4
    ◊ J 10 7
    ♣ Q J 9 8 5 3 2

What rebid would you select in the following auctions?

	OPENER	RESPONDER
	1NT	2♣
	?	

17. ♠ 8 7 3 2
    ♡ A Q
    ◊ K 10 6
    ♣ A J 10 4

18. ♠ A 10 7
    ♡ K 4
    ◊ A J 8
    ♣ Q 10 9 5 3

	OPENER	RESPONDER
	1NT	2♣
	2♡	?

19. ♠ A Q 10 7
    ♡ 8 5
    ◊ K Q 4
    ♣ Q 10 5 2

20. ♠ A J 10 4
    ♡ Q 7
    ◊ K 10 4
    ♣ J 7 6 3

	OPENER	RESPONDER
	1NT	3 ♡
	?	

21. ♠ K J 10 3
   ♡ J 10
   ◇ A Q 9
   ♣ Q 10 7 4

22. ♠ A J 5 2
   ♡ 4 3 2
   ◇ A 10 9 2
   ♣ A J

Partner opens 2NT; what initial response would you make with the following hands?

23. ♠ K J 10 9 5
   ♡ 4 2
   ◇ J 10 7
   ♣ 9 8 5

24. ♠ 5
   ♡ Q 10 9 5
   ◇ Q 6 5 3 2
   ♣ J 10 6

25. ♠ K 10 7
   ♡ 7 6
   ◇ Q J 10 5
   ♣ K J 7 4

26. ♠ K Q 10 9 5 3
   ♡ 3
   ◇ K 10 9 3
   ♣ K 6

27. ♠ 7 4
   ♡ K 10 9 6 5 3
   ◇ J 10 2
   ♣ 8 7

Answers
Exercise #2

1. 1 ♠
Never open 1NT when your hand contains a five-card major.

2. 1NT
The best description of this semi-balanced 15 count with a weak five-card minor.

3. 1 ♣
No other choice — 16 HCP!

4. 1 ♣
Intending to rebid 2NT which will describe a balanced 19-21 count. This hand is a point light for a 2NT opening.

5. 1 ◇
Despite the weakness of your six-card suit and balanced strength (stoppers in all suits), it is best to open 1 ◇, not 1NT, when you have a six-card minor.

6. 2NT
Meets all the requirements for a 2NT opening.

7. 1NT
Do not consider opening 1 ♠ even though you have the best four-card suit possible. As we shall discuss in the next chapter, opening 1 ♡ or 1 ♠ always promises a five-card suit and this rule should never be broken.

8. 2 ♣
Use the Stayman Convention to explore for a possible 4-4 major suit fit. If opener rebids 2 ◇ (stating he does not have a four-card major), jump to 3NT with your game-going values. Over either 2 ♡ or 2 ♠ you should jump directly to game in the major suit partner shows.

9. 2NT
Invitational.

10. 3 ♠
Forcing to game giving opener a choice of contracts. With three or four spades, opener will raise to 4 ♠ and with a doubleton spade opener should sign-off in 3NT.

11. 4♠
Your side has at least an eight-card spade fit and sufficient values for game, with slam out of reach according to the Limited Bid Strategy. Bid what you think you can make.

12. 2♠
Sign-off in 2♠; this pitiful hand might not produce a trick for partner in 1NT but should take a few tricks with spades as trump. Remember, 2◇, 2♡, or 2♠ over 1NT are in no way constructive; they simply inform partner that the hand will play better in a suit than 1NT.

13. 4NT
Quantitative raise (not to be confused with the Blackwood Convention asking for aces). Opener is urged to bid a slam if he has more than a minimum 1NT opening.

14. 3◇
100% forcing to game showing an unbalanced hand with a good, long suit. May have slam interest.

15. 6NT
With partner holding 13-15 HCP a small slam in notrump should be certain, and a grand slam is out of reach using the Limited Bid Strategy.

16. 2♣
Although partner will initially believe you are interested in locating a major suit fit (properly assuming that 2♣ is the Stayman Convention), you intend to sign-off in 3♣ after opener's rebid, clarifying your hand. Remember, a direct jump to 3♣ would be game-forcing, so the only way to sign-off in 3♣ is to use 2♣ (the Stayman Convention) as a vehicle.

17. 2♠
Responder did not ask you whether you had a *good* four-card major, only if you had a four-card major, which you do have.

18. 2◇
Informing partner that you do not have a four-card major. 2◇ promises no particular length or strength in diamonds.

19. 3NT
If opener has both four hearts and four spades, he will correct 3NT to 4♠, knowing you would not have used the Stayman Convention without four cards in one of the majors (obviously not hearts in light of your 3NT rebid).

20. 2NT
Invitational, but not forcing. This rebid describes the values for a direct raise to 2NT with a four-card major.

21. 3NT
Responder is asking opener to choose between 4♡ and 3NT, depending on his heart support. With only a doubleton heart, you should rebid 3NT. 3♡ is forcing to game.

22. 4♡
Partner's jump to 3♡ promises at least a five-card suit, giving your side a minimum of eight hearts. With three card support (even the 432), you should raise hearts.

23. 3♠
Showing a reasonable five-card suit, giving opener a choice between 3NT and 4♠ depending on his spade length.

24. 3♣
The Stayman Convention, hoping in this case to locate a four-four heart fit. Responder intends to rebid 3NT if opener doesn't rebid 3♡.

25. 4NT
Quantitative raise asking opener to raise to 6NT with more than a minimum 2NT opening.

26. 4♣
The Gerber Convention asking for aces. With a fine six-card suit the only question to be resolved is "How High," which will depend on the number of aces and kings opener holds.

27. 4♡
Bid what you think you can make. 4♡ is a sign-off over 2NT as it is over 1NT. The partnership has a minimum of eight hearts and you have sufficient assets for game.

Chapter 5

Major Suit Openings

BEFORE DISCUSSING these major suit opening bids in depth, bear in mind two important principles.

1. The high-card strength is strictly limited. Since we open all hands of 16 or more HCP with 1 ♣, the precise range of a 1 ♡ or 1 ♠ opening is 11-15.

2. Opening 1 ♡ or 1 ♠ in any position promises at least a five-card suit.

"Five ever; four never"

So that it is easy to locate an eight-card fit in either major suit, 1 ♡ and 1 ♠ openings *always* promise at least a five-card suit. Although AKQJ may be a far more useful trump suit than J5432, do not consider opening the bidding with one of a major, even with such powerful four-card holdings. By the same token, it is perfectly acceptable to open the bidding with 65432 of spades or hearts if you hold the overall strength for an opening bid.

Some five-card major advocates suggest that it is reasonable to open a good four-card major in third or fourth position with a minimum or subminimum opener. Playing Precision this is NOT recommended. Limited opening bids are the same in all positions. The partner of a third or fourth seat Precision opening should always respond as though partner had full values for his limited opening bid. And this includes a holding of five hearts or spades when the opening bid is one of a major.

When you hold two five-card suits, you should always open the higher ranking suit, irrespective of the relative strength of the two suits. Six-five hands should be opened in the six-card suit with one exception.

With a relatively weak six-card minor suit it is usually best to open one of your five-card major. As examples:

(a) ♠ J 8 6 3 2   ♡ A K Q 10 3   ◊ Q 10   ♣ 7

Open 1 ♠ (even though your five-card heart suit is far stronger).

(b) ♠ A K J 10 9   ♡ Q 6 5 4 3 2   ◊ –   ♣ K 8

Open 1 ♡. (Only with a six-card minor suit and a five-card major should you consider opening your five-card suit. Holding six-five in the majors, always open your longest suit.)

(c) ♠ A 6   ♡ K Q J 10 7   ◊ Q 8 5 4 3 2   ♣ –

Open 1 ♡ in light of your weak six-card diamond holding.

(d) ♠ K 10 9 4 2   ♡ 3   ◊ A K J 10 7 4   ♣ J

Open the bidding 1 ◊, not 1 ♠. With an exceptional six-card minor you should not distort your distribution.

Strength: clearly defined "ceilings" and "floors"

Bridge is a bidder's game. And Precision is designed for those who love to bid. The side that strikes the first blow in the auction has a decided advantage if the auction becomes competitive.

Consequently, we have lowered the standard requirements for opening the bidding. Most hands with 11 high card points justify an opening bid, particularly when you hold a five-card major. Aggressive bidding is the cornerstone of Precision bidding, and the key to its success. Of course, to be a winner you must also play and defend well, but, at the bridge table, most players win or lose in the bidding.

Consider the following hand:

♠ K 9 8 3 2   ♡ A Q 5   ◊ Q 8 7 6   ♣ 2

Although there might be considerable danger in entering the auction *after* your opponents open the bidding, playing Precision there is relatively little risk in an opening bid with this type of hand. Remember, your hand is limited to 15 HCP by your failure to open 1 ♣.

Although the range of a Precision 1 ♡ or 1 ♠ opening is 11-15, the minimum strength cannot be defined strictly in terms of high-card points. The quality and location of your points, your distribution, and your overall playing strength are important considerations in determining whether you should open a marginal hand. Since you must hold at least a five-card major to consider opening 1 ♡ or 1 ♠, we tend to open minimum hands in the majors more often than we do in the minors. Our general rule is to open ALL 12 point hands containing a five-card major and most 11's with any texture or distributional assets beyond 5-3-3-2. We would open all of the following minimum hands:

(a) ♠ K Q 10 9 6   ♡ 8 7 4   ◇ A Q 10 5   ♣ 3

(b) ♠ 10 9 6   ♡ A J 10 7 5   ◇ 8   ♣ K Q J 2

(c) ♠ 6 5 4 3 2   ♡ K Q 10   ◇ A Q 10   ♣ 9 8

(d) ♠ Q   ♡ Q 10 8 6 5   ◇ A K 10 2   ♣ J 7 6

(e) ♠ A K 5 4 2   ♡ 6 5   ◇ Q J   ♣ Q 4 3 2

(f) ♠ A K 7   ♡ 10 9 5 3 2   ◇ A 10 4   ♣ 8 5

With exceptional distribution and your honors concentrated in your long suits, we might advise opening the bidding on even less than 11 HCP. For example:

(a) ♠ K J 10 9 3   ♡ A Q 10 9 6   ◇ 9 8 3   ♣ —

(b) ♠ A J 10 9 3   ♡ 10 9 7   ◇ —   ♣ A J 10 7 4

(c) ♠ J 10   ♡ A 10 9 6 3   ◇ 5   ♣ A J 10 7 2

When illustration (c) was opened 1 ♡ during a highly competitive rubber bridge game, a fine score resulted. The complete deal and auction being:

DEALER: N
VUL: Both

NORTH
♠ J 10
♡ A 10 9 6 2
◇ 5
♣ A J 10 7 2

WEST
♠ A 9 7 6 4
♡ Q
◇ A Q 9
♣ Q 8 5 3

EAST
♠ K Q 3 2
♡ 7 5
◇ K 8 7 3
♣ K 6 4

```
                    SOUTH
                    ♠ 8 5
                    ♡ K J 8 4 3
                    ◇ J 10 6 4 2
                    ♣ 9
      NORTH     EAST     SOUTH     WEST
      1 ♡       Pass     4 ♡       Pass
      Pass      Pass
```

North's light opening bid at favorable vulnerability, coupled with South's tactical raise to game, enabled us to level the score on a hand where our opponents could have won the rubber if they had bid 4 ♠ and been allowed to play there. It is difficult to fault either East or West for not getting into the bidding. East's pass of 1 ♡ is certainly normal, and at this vulnerability with a passing partner, any action by West could easily be catastrophic.

Despite our fondness for "striking the first blow in the auction," some 11 point hands should not be opened, even though they include a five-card major. Reluctantly, we would pass holding:

(a) ♠ J 5 4 3 2   ♡ Q J   ◇ K 9 5 3   ♣ K J

Our lack of quick tricks and the concentration of honors in our short suits recommend a pass with this 11 count.

(b) ♠ K Q   ♡ Q 6 5 2   ◇ K J   ♣ 9 8 5 3

Here again we both lack defensive strength and have no compensating distributional features. It is best to pass.

(c) ♠ Q J 7 6 2   ♡ Q J 8   ◇ Q J   ♣ Q J 2

Although we advise opening all 12 point hands, we would pass with this particular hand which is far better suited for pinochle than bridge. You should have some defensive strength when you open the bidding, and this hand has little or none.

When you are dealt a marginal opening bid, a good rule of thumb is to open when you have two quick tricks and pass if you do not.

Responding to 1 ♡ and 1 ♠

As discussed in the opening chapters, trying to respond accurately to a Standard American opening bid of one of a suit can be highly frustrating. If (as responder) you're looking at a puny 5, 6, or 7 point hand and decide to avoid getting too high by passing, you may find that you've missed a lay-down game because partner has a 20 point powerhouse. If instead you elect to scrape up a response, partner may get overly excited, bid too much, and hand your opponents a large penalty.

In Precision, however, you are never faced with this problem. Partner cannot have more than 15 HCP when he opens 1 ♡ or 1 ♠. There is no need to strain to keep the bidding open with a weak hand. Therefore, you can confidently pass with 0-7 points.

Raising 1 ♡ and 1 ♠

Because a high priority in Precision is given to locating and establishing a major suit fit, your first duty as responder after a 1 ♡ or 1 ♠ opening is to raise partner's suit if you have support. Three-card support (even 432) is adequate since the opener MUST have a five-card suit. The way you choose to raise opener's major depends entirely on the strength and distribution of your hand. In determining your strength, remember when you raise (or plan to raise) partner's suit, you should add to your HCP what we have termed Distribution Points (DP) as follows:

Void:	5
Singleton:	3
Doubleton:	1

The total of your HCP and DP determines how high you should raise. The following table outlines all of the Precision raises over 1 ♡ and 1 ♠ openings.

After 1 ♡ or 1 ♠		
Responder bids:	Description:	Supporting Points:*
2♡, 2♠	At least three-card support with no more than 10 points in support of opener's suit.	8-10
3♡, 3♠	Limit raise (invitational but not forcing). Good three-card support (Qxx or better).	11-13
4♡, 4♠	Either: (a) pre-emptive raise to game with with long trump support, (ex. 4♠ over 1♠: ♠Q10743 ♡6 ◊AJ8532 ♣8);	No specific range

*Combination of HCP and DP.

> or, (b), game-going values (14 to a bad 16
> points in support) with NO interest in slam.
> (Ex. 4♡ over 1♡ holdng ♠KQ10
> ♡KQ93 ◊Q842 ♣Q2.) Opener should
> PASS direct raises to game in either case.

There are only two occasions when you might not choose some form of
initial raise with support for partner's opening major suit:

(1) With an invitational hand (11 or 12 HCP) containing a reasonably
good side-suit or a concentration of values in a side suit. For example:

♠ 10 9 3   ♡ Q 10 9   ◊ 9 8   ♣ A K J 10 7

OPENER	RESPONDER
1♡	?

Instead of making a direct limit raise to 3♡, it is best to bid 2♣ over 1♡
and then make an invitational delayed raise in hearts. Opener will have
more information in determining your side's prospects for game,
knowing you have a good club suit along with your support for hearts. If
you side-suit is weaker, however, you are best advised to make a direct
limit raise. For example:

♠ K J 10   ♡ K Q 10   ◊ 8 7   ♣ Q 5 4 3 2

Raise 1♡ directly to 3♡.

(2) When you are interested in slam and wish to introduce your side
suit to elicit more information about opener's hand. For example:

♠ K J 7 6   ♡ A 7   ◊ J 10   ♣ A K Q 10 9

OPENER	RESPONDER
1♠	?

This powerful responding hand is best described by an immediate jump
shift to 3♣. Alert opener to your slam interest immediately; then
support spades with your rebid. A small slam is more than likely and a
grand slam is possible, even if partner holds a minimum opening bid.

Outside of these two rare exceptions, it is usually best to raise
partner's major suit opening whenever you have adequate trump
support. The reason is simple. After a raise, the opener is usually able to

judge the final contract. Such auctions are simple, direct, and precise. Raising opener's major not only resolves WHERE the hand should be played on most deals; also it clearly defines responder's strength, simplifying the questions of HOW HIGH. It becomes a simple matter for the opener to use the "Limited Bid Strategy."

The bidding rule of 11

When responder lacks support for opener's suit, his choice of responses is limited by his strength. In order to bid a new suit at the two-level, responder must have 11 HCP. With less than 11 points, the only new suit responder can bid over a major suit opening is 1♠ over 1♡. Although in principle any response over a limited opening bid suggests a minimum of eight points (since you could pass with 0-7), you might elect to bid 1♠ over 1♡ with slightly less if your hand is unsuitable for a heart contract. We would respond 1♠ over a 1♡ opening with either:

(a) ♠ K J 10 5 2   ♡ 4 2   ◇ K 7 4   ♣ 10 9 4

or

(b) ♠ K Q 10 9   ♡ 7   ◇ 6 3 2   ♣ J 10 9 5 2

Hand (a) has slim prospects for game unless partner has a maximum limited opener with a good spade fit; holding (b), it is very likely we have a better resting place than 1♡.

Following this bidding "rule of 11," no matter how good or long your suit is, you cannot directly introduce that suit at the two-level without 11 points (or an exceptional 10 count with a fine suit that you choose to inflate to 11 points). For example, you should not bid 2♣ over 1♡ with either of the following hands:

(a) ♠ 4 3   ♡ 9 8 5   ◇ 6 2   ♣ A K J 10 5 2

or

(b) ♠ J 10 4   ♡ 7 6   ◇ Q 8   ♣ K Q J 9 7 4

With (a), you should simply raise 1♡ to 2♡, describing your three-card heart support and 8-10 supporting points; and with (b) your correct call is 1NT, since you can neither support hearts nor introduce your fine club suit immediately.

When you are considering bidding either minor suit over a 1 ♡ or 1 ♠ opener, there are no requirements as to either the length (four is sufficient) or strength of the suit you bid, provided you have the required 11 HCP. On the other hand, bidding 2 ♡ over 1 ♠ should promise a five-card suit, since it will make it easier to locate a good major suit fit and partner will know he can raise with three-card support.

Notrump responses to 1 ♡ and 1 ♠

Precision notrump responses to major suit openings are similar in range to Precision raises. Needless to repeat, you cannot count any distributional points since you are not raising partner's suit. The following table outlines the Precision notrump steps:

Over 1 ♡ and 1 ♠		
Responder Bids:	**Description:**	**HCP:**
1NT	Denies three-card support for opener's suit and four spades over 1 ♡. May not be a balanced hand since responder does not have the required 11 HCP for a 2 over 1 new suit response.	8-10
2NT	INVITATIONAL and non-forcing. Promises a balanced hand with scattered strength. Denies three-card support for opener's major.	11-13
3NT	Balanced hand with scattered strength. Denies three-card support for opener's major.	14-16

You may note that these ranges are a bit different from those used in standard bidding methods. The reason is the limited nature of the opening bid.

Since partner may have as little as 11 or 12 points when he opens 1 ♡ or 1 ♠, 2NT can no longer be a forcing response based on 12 or 13 points. Therefore, use 2NT to describe a balanced 11-13 point hand where game should be bid only if partner has more than minimum values for his opening bid. Over 2NT, opener is invited to carry on to game with more than a minimum Precision opener, but is permitted to pass if he has opened a poor 11 or 12 point hand. In this respect, 2NT is similar to a direct limit raise (3 ♡ over 1 ♡ or 3 ♠ over 1 ♠) since in both auctions opener is invited to carry on to game only with more than minimum values. In neither case is opener *forced* to bid again. We would respond 2NT over an opening 1 ♡ bid with either of the following:

     (a) ♠ K 10 2 ♡ J 10 ◇ K J 10 5 ♣ Q J 10 9

or

     (b) ♠ A J 8 ♡ 9 8 ◇ Q J 9 3 ♣ K J 7 4

With either (a) or (b) we would expect to make game if partner can bid it, and a part score is very likely the limit of the hand if partner passes. Notice how easy this makes the problem of what to bid on hands that are close to a forcing 2NT response in Standard American.

When responder has sufficient assets to force the bidding to game but lacks any interest in slam, holding a balanced hand with scattered strength simply make a direct jump to 3NT. Opener may elect to "correct" 3NT to four of his major if he holds six or more cards in his suit, knowing that responder has at least two. Opener may also bid or suggest a minor suit game or slam with a highly distributional hand unsuited for 3NT. In short, 3NT need not end the auction as is frequently known as "game-closing". Responder is simply saying that the partnership has sufficient strength for game and he has a balanced hand.

Jump shifts

Playing Precision, it is never necessary to jump shift simply because you hold a lot of points. With strong two or three-suited hands, often you cannot afford to consume bidding space with a jump shift. Consequently, jump shifts are used on only two types of responding hands:

(1) A powerful single-suited hand with a self-sufficient trump suit. Definite slam interest.

(2) A fine supporting hand for partner's opening suit, with an excellent side-suit that promises to produce a number of tricks after trumps are drawn. (In this case you intend to jump shift in your "side-suit" and then support partner's suit.)

Over an opening 1 ♠ bid we would jump shift to 3 ♣ with either of the following hands:

(a)   ♠ A 3   ♡ K Q 7   ◇ 6   ♣ A K Q J 10 7 2

or

(b)   ♠ K Q 10 3   ♡ –   ◇ A 9 8   ♣ A K J 5 3 2

But we would NOT jump shift over 1 ♠ holding either:

(c)   ♠ 9 3   ♡ K   ◇ A K Q 10 4   ♣ A K 10 3 2

or

(d)   ♠ A Q   ♡ A K   ◇ K 10 7 3 2   ♣ K 10 5 3

Even though slam is a distinct possibility with either (c) or (d), you have no idea "WHERE" your partnership should play this deal. The space consumed by a jump shift with either of these hands hinders your attempt to locate the best final contract. Your best response with both (c) and (d) is simply to bid 2 ◇ and await developments.

Remember, a Precision jump shift should never be based solely on high card strength. Effective jump shifts are based on the ability to guide the auction to WHERE the hand should be played.

We have now considered all of the initial Precision responses to a major suit opening, as well as the basic requirements to open 1 ♡ or 1 ♠.

Rebids by opener

Limiting the strength of the opening bid and in most cases the initial response eliminates the need for a large number of forcing rebids. In Precision, almost all of opener's rebids and most of responder's rebids should be non-forcing. There is rarely any reason for long, complicated, involved (and often confusing) auctions. Precision is designed to answer the question WHERE early in the auction, and the LIMITED-BID STRATEGY should clarify HOW HIGH.

Major suit game tries by opener:

Once a major suit fit is established, the only remaining question to be resolved in the auction is HOW HIGH. When responder makes a simple raise of opener's major (showing 8-10 points in support), unless opener holds a maximum limited opener the partnership should settle for a part-score. And even if the opener holds a maximum, game is by no means certain since he can hold no more than 15 points and partner might hold as little as 8. Consequently, with a maximum the opener should not jump to game but make some form of "game try," leaving the decision to responder, who knows whether he holds a minimum or maximum simple raise.

We suggest three different types of game tries by the opener after a simple major suit raise:

(1) A BID IN A NEW SUIT. This is the suit in which opener needs help. Responder should accept the "help" game try with either extreme shortness or a concentration of strength in the new suit. Ax or Kx are particularly good holdings to accept partner's game try, since you have both high card strength and relative shortness. For example:

OPENER	RESPONDER
1♠	2♠
3♣	

Opener should make a game try in clubs with either:

(a) ♠ K Q 10 9 3   ♡ A   ◇ A 10 9   ♣ Q 10 4 2

or

(b) ♠ A J 10 7 4 3   ♡ A Q   ◇ K 2   ♣ J 7 6

After a new suit game try, responder can:

(a) *Sign-off in three of the agreed major* with no interest in game. (This shows either a minimum raise or a poor holding in the new suit, such as xxx or Jxxx.) After raising spades, responder should refuse a game try in diamonds holding either:

(1) ♠ K J 7 5   ♡ K 10 4   ◇ 7 6 3 2   ♣ 9 8

or

(2) ♠ 7 5 3   ♡ A J 4 2   ◇ Q 5 2   ♣ J 8 6

(b) *Bid game in the agreed major* with either a maximum raise or a particularly good holding in the new suit bid by opener. After raising hearts, responder would accept a game try in clubs with either of the following hands:

(3) ♠ 7 6   ♡ J 10 6 5   ◇ 10 9 8 6 3   ♣ A K

or

(4) ♠ 10 9 5   ♡ Q 10 4 2   ◇ K Q 10 3 2   ♣ 5

(c) *Bid a new suit below the three-level* of opener's major with a concentration of values in that suit, interest in game, but not quite enough strength or a good enough holding in partner's second suit to go directly to game. After raising hearts, responder might bid 3 ◇ over a 3 ♣ game try with either:

(5) ♠ 8 7 3   ♡ Q 10 7   ◇ A Q 10 5 4   ♣ J 6

or

(6) ♠ 9 7 4   ♡ J 10 6 3   ◇ A K 10 9   ♣ 10 9

It is now up to the opener to make the decision whether the partnership should bid a game.

(2) REBID 2NT. This describes a 5-3-3-2 hand with 15 good HCP and scattered strength. Responder is then given five choices:

(a) *Pass 2NT* with a balanced minimum response usually holding only three-card trump support.

(b) *Sign-off in three of the agreed major* with minimum values and a hand better adapted for play in a suit than notrump.

(c) *Jump to four of the agreed major* with maximum values, knowing that all of his high cards will be working since opener must have 5-3-3-2 distribution.

(d) *Bid 3NT* with a balanced maximum well-adapted for the notrump game. (This is one of the rare occasions when you might elect to play notrump after discovering an eight-card major suit fit.)

(e) *Introduce a new suit at the three-level,* showing a concentration of values in that suit, leaving the decision to opener as to what the final contract should be. Similar to bidding a new suit over opener's new suit game try showing definite interest in game.

(3) RAISE TO THREE OF THE AGREED UPON MAJOR. Since (1) and (2) are available as game tries when you need help in a specific suit or hold a balanced maximum, you can use a rebid in the agreed suit, inquiring about responder's holding in the trump suit. In short, the hand is likely to produce a game if responder has good trump support, ir-

respective of the overall strength of his raise. We would bid 3 ♡ over responder's 2 ♡ raise with either:

(a) ♠ A K 10   ♡ J 10 4 3 2   ◊ A K 10 9   ♣ 3

or

(b) ♠ A J   ♡ Q 9 6 5 2   ◊ 4   ♣ A K J 7 3

Both hands offer excellent prospects for game if responder has good trump support and little else. Responder should happily accept partner's game try of 3 ♡ if he has raised 1 ♡ to 2 ♡ holding:

(c) ♠ 9 8 5   ♡ A K 8 7   ◊ 8 7 5 3   ♣ 4 2

But he should not consider bidding 4 ♡ if he has made a simple raise with:

(d) ♠ K 6 3   ♡ 8 7 4   ◊ Q J 105   ♣ K J 2

(This rule applies despite responder's maximum raise with (d) and minimum with (c).)

Chapter 6

Rebids by Responder
MAJOR SUIT GAME TRIES

IN ADDITION TO opener's three types of game tries after his major suit is raised, responder may wish to make a game try when opener raises his 1 ♠ *response* to 2 ♠. With invitational values, responder has three choices:

(1) BID 2NT. This describes an 11-13 point balanced hand with stoppers in the unbid suits.

Opener may then:

(a) *Pass 2NT* with a semi-balanced minimum and no interest in game, figuring that eight tricks may be the limit of the hand.

(b) *Sign-off at 3 ♠* with a minimum opener better suited for a trump contract than notrump.

(c) *Jump to 4 ♠* with maximum values for his previous 2 ♠ raise.

(d) *Bid 3NT* with a semi-balanced maximum and scattered strength well-suited for the notrump game in spite of the major suit fit. Perhaps nine tricks are the limit of the hand.

(e) *Introduce a new suit at the three-level or rebid 3 ♡*. This is intended to give responder additional information about opener's hand in order to find the best final contract.

(2) RAISE TO 3 ♠. Responder is asking opener to continue on to game if he has good trump support. This is designed to cover those hands where game is likely if you can avoid two or three trump losers. For example:

OPENER	RESPONDER
1 ♡	1 ♠
2 ♠	??

We would bid 3 ♠ with either:

(a) ♠ J 10 5 4   ♡ J 10   ◇ A K J 10 2   ♣ 8 5

or

(b) ♠ Q 4 3 2   ♡ K 5   ◇ A J 10 6   ♣ J 10 4

Either (a) or (b) should have an excellent play for game if opener holds good trump support for spades. Opener should accept responder's game try of 3 ♠ if he has raised to 2 ♠ holding:

(c) ♠ A Q 10 5   ♡ A Q 10 7 2   ◇ 10 9 7   ♣ 8

But, even though he has almost a maximum limited opener, he should *not* raise to game with:

(d) ♠ J 7 3 2   ♡ K Q J 4 2   ◇ K 5   ♣ K J

(3) BID 3♡ OR A NEW SUIT AT THE THREE-LEVEL. When responder bids 3♣ or 3◇, this is the suit in which responder needs help. Knowing partner needs help in the new suit bid, opener may elect to:

(a) *Sign-off in 3♠* with no interest in game.

(b) *Jump to 4♠.* Showing either maximum values for his previous bidding or a particularly good holding in the new suit bid by partner.

(c) *Bid a suit below 3♠* with a concentration of values in that suit but not quite enough strength to justify committing the hand to game directly over partner's game try.

Since new suits by responder are 100% forcing after a major suit fit has been established, they may be the start of a slam try. Although initially opener will respond as though partner was making a game try, consider the following auction:

OPENER		RESPONDER	
	1♡		1♠
	2♠		3♣ (Most likely a game try in spades)
(Rejected)	3♠		4◇ (Obviously a SLAM try since you could sign off in 4♠, if that was your limit)

Other rebids by opener after a new suit response

When responder makes a forcing bid in a new suit after you've opened 1♡ or 1♠, clarify the strength and nature of your opening bid by choosing your rebid as follows:

(1) WITH A MINIMUM OPENING BID (11-14 HCP):

(a) *Make a single raise of responder's suit.*

(b) *Bid a new four-card or longer suit.*

(c) *Bid notrump as cheaply as possible.*

(d) *Rebid your major suit as cheaply as possible.*

(2) WITH A MAXIMUM OPENING BID (14+ or 15 HCP):

(a) *Make a jump raise of responder's suit.*

(b) *Bid a new four-card or longer suit.*

(c) *Jump in notrump* with a balanced hand and stoppers in the unbid suits.

(d) *Jump rebid your major suit* if it has six or more cards.

(e) *Jump shift* with 5-5 distribution or better.

Since opener has defined his hand very precisely with his first and second bid in the auction, responder can and should pass if he can tell that game is out of the question and the contract is a playable one — even if this means passing a strong-sounding rebid that would be forcing in standard bidding, such as a jump rebid either in notrump or in one of your suits.

If responder has no interest in game but opener's rebid is unplayable, he can simply correct the contract to a playable contract and opener is expected to pass. For example:

	OPENER	RESPONDER
(1)	1♡	1♠
	1NT	??

Responder holds:

♠ K J 10 4   ♡ 3 2   ◇ 7   ♣ Q J 10 6 4 3

Responder should "correct" 1NT to 2♣ which opener is expected to pass. Simple new suit rebids are non-forcing after a 1NT rebid by opener.

	OPENER	RESPONDER
(2)	1♡	1NT
	2♡	??

Responder holds:

♠ Q 10 2   ♡ —   ◇ K Q J 10 7 2   ♣ 10 9 6 3

Responder should bid 3◇ over 2♡ having limited his strength by his initial 1NT response. (Responder could not introduce diamonds initially since 2 ◇ over 1 ♡ would have promised 11 points.) After a limiting 1NT response, new suits by responder are not forcing; indeed, opener is expected to pass.

(3)	OPENER	RESPONDER
	1♡	1♠
	2♣	??

Responder holds:

♠ K 10 9 3   ♡ 6   ◇ K Q 10 9 5 2   ♣ 8 5

Responder should bid 2 ◇ over 2♣. Playing Precision a simple new suit rebid at the two-level is NON-FORCING.

There is no reason to use any of these rebids by responder as forcing since opener's hand is limited.

If responder wishes to make a forcing bid after opener's simple rebid, he must:

(1) *Jump in a new suit.* For example:

OPENER	RESPONDER
1♡	1♠
1NT	3♣
	(Forcing)

Responder might hold:

♠ K J 10 6 3   ♡ J 10   ◇ 7   ♣ A K J 10 3

(2) *Bid a new suit at the three-level.* For example:

OPENER	RESPONDER
1♡	1♠
2◇	3♣
	(Forcing)

Responder might hold:

♠ A Q 9 8 3   ♡ 9   ◇ J 8   ♣ A Q 10 7 6

(3) *Bid a new suit after making a 2 over 1 response.* For example:

<pre>
            OPENER   RESPONDER
              1♠   2♣
              2♦   2♥
                           (Forcing)
</pre>

Responder might hold:

♠ Q 10   ♡ A 10 9 3   ◇ J 10   ♣ A Q 10 9 6

(4) *Jump raise one of opener's suits* (below game) or *make a jump rebid in his own suit* after a two over one response. For example:

<pre>
(a)   OPENER   RESPONDER
              1♠   2♣
              2♦   4♦
                           (Forcing)
</pre>

Responder might hold:

♠ 10 9   ♡ 6   ◇ K Q J 7   ♣ A K J 10 4 3

<pre>
(b)   OPENER   RESPONDER
              1♠   2♣
              2♦   4♣
                           (Forcing)
</pre>

Responder might hold:

♠ Q 3   ♡ A   ◇ 10 9 4   ♣ A K J 10 7 5 2

<pre>
(c)   OPENER   RESPONDER
              1♠   2♣
              2♡   3♠
                           (Forcing)
</pre>

Responder might hold:

♠ J 10 3   ♡ K 4   ◇ 8 5   ♣ A K Q 6 3 2

If responder lacks the values for a forcing rebid but has definite interest in game, he may elect to make an invitational rebid. The following rebids are all invitational, but NON-FORCING:

(1) *Jump to three of opener's major or his own.* For example:

(a) OPENER   RESPONDER
     1♡   1♠
     1NT   3♡
                 (Invitational, but not
                 (forcing)

Responder might hold:

♠ A Q J 10 7   ♡ J 3 2   ◇ Q 10 9   ♣ 8 7

(b) OPENER   RESPONDER
     1♡   1♠
     2♣   3♠
                 (Invitational, but not
                 forcing)

Responder might hold:

♠ K Q J 10 6 2   ♡ 7 5   ◇ A 10 7   ♣ 6 3

(Note: Jump rebids in responder's first bid suit always promise a reasonably good six-card suit.)

(2) *Raise opener's 1NT rebid to 2NT after making a 2 over 1 response.* For example:

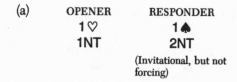

(a) OPENER   RESPONDER
     1♡   1♠
     1NT   2NT
                 (Invitational, but not
                 forcing)

Responder might hold:

♠ J 10 8 5   ♡ Q J   ◇ K 10 6 3   ♣ A 9 2

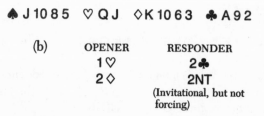

(b) OPENER   RESPONDER
     1♡   2♣
     2◇   2NT
                 (Invitational, but not
                 forcing)

Responder might hold:

♠ K J 10   ♡ 8 7   ◊ 9 4 2   ♣ A Q J 9 3

(3) *Make a simple raise of a suit bid by opener.* For example:

(a)	OPENER	RESPONDER
	1♠	2♣
	2♡	3♡
		(Invitational, but not forcing)

Responder might hold:

♠ 9 4   ♡ Q 10 6 3   ◊ K 10   ♣ A Q 5 3 2

(b)	OPENER	RESPONDER
	1♡	1♠
	2♡	3♡
		(Invitational, but not forcing)

Responder might hold:

♠ A K 10 4 2   ♡ J 10   ◊ Q 10 9 5   ♣ 9 8

(In this auction opener has implied a six-card heart suit, so J10 double-ton is more than adequate support.)

(c)	OPENER	RESPONDER
	1♡	1♠
	2◊	3◊
		(Invitational, but not forcing)

Responder might hold:

♠ K Q 10 6 3   ♡ 8 5   ◊ A 10 9 3   ♣ J 4

Subsequent bidding after a notrump response

When responder makes an initial notrump response which describes his point count very precisely, the opener rarely has any rebid problems. If the opener's hand is semi-balanced it is a simple matter of using the Limited Bid Strategy to decide whether to sign-off by passing or raise to game. Over a 1NT response, game is out of the question unless opener holds a 15 point maximum limited opener, and in that event he should invite game by bidding 2NT.

There is never any reason for opener to rebid a five-card major suit, since all notrump responses deny holding three-card support for opener's suit. Therefore, if opener does rebid his suit, it promises at least a six-card suit.

After a 1NT response the opener should always introduce a second suit if he has one. (The only exception: 2 ♠ after opening 1 ♡, since responder has already denied holding four spades.) Even with 5-4-2-2 distribution it is best to bid your other suit. Remember, responder's hand may not be balanced when he responds 1NT. Partner may be anxiously awaiting the opportunity to show a long, reasonably good suit which he could not bid directly, since he lacked the required 11 points for a two over one response.

Over an invitational (non-forcing) jump to 2NT, the opener knows responder's hand is both balanced and that he holds a doubleton in opener's major. (With three-card support he would have made a limit raise showing the same 11-13 points.) Consequently, with a six-card or longer major the opener should rebid his suit at the three level with a minimum 11 or 12 HCP or jump to game in his suit with a maximum. For example:

	(a)	OPENER	RESPONDER
		1 ♡	2NT
		??	

Holding:

♠ A 10 6   ♡ K J 10 8 5 2   ◊ A Q   ♣ 10 9

Opener should jump to 4 ♡.

	(b)	OPENER	RESPONDER
		1 ♠	2NT
		??	

Holding:

♠ A Q 9 5 3 2   ♡ K Q 10   ◇ 9 8   ♣ 7 4

Opener should sign-off by simply rebidding 3 ♠.

Moving up to 3 and 4 notrump responses, the question is no longer whether the partnership should be in game but rather which game you should bid. Since responder's strength and distribution are defined within narrow limits, opener rarely has any problems. Obviously, new suits over 3NT but below the game level are forcing and suggest that opener has a considerably unbalanced hand that will play better in a suit than notrump.

After a jump shift

An immediate jump shift by responder shows definite slam interest. You will recall that responder must either have a self-sufficient trump suit or an excellent fit for opener's suit with a good side-suit.

Since partner is interested in slam, it is very important that opener clarify even further the nature of his limited opening bid. With a semi-balanced (5-3-3-2 distribution) opening bid, the opener should usually elect to make a simple rebid in notrump. Holding a more distributional opener the following calls are available:

(1) *Rebid a six-card or longer major suit.*

(2) *Support partner's suit.* Either doubleton honor or three small are more than ample support since responder has shown a fine suit.

(3) *Show a reasonably good side four-card suit.* (Although it is perfectly acceptable to bid a relatively weak second suit in most auctions, you should avoid bidding weak suits after partner has jump shifted.)

(4) *Jump in your suit* if it is solid (AKQxx or better).

(5) *Jump shift in response* with at least a good five-five two-suiter, with most of your strength concentrated in your two suits. (Your reason for jumping is simply to describe your distribution, NOT to show you have a maximum limited opener.)

After responder makes an immediate jump shift, most auctions should be fairly simple and direct if opener keeps in mind that partner must hold one of two types of hands. Consider this deal played in a recent rubber bridge game:

DEALER: N
VUL: Both

NORTH
♠ A K Q J 7
♡ J 10 5
◇ 10 9 4
♣ 8 6

WEST
♠ 10 8 4 3
♡ K Q
◇ K 8 7 5 2
♣ 10 3

EAST
♠ 6 5
♡ 8 7 6 4 2
◇ Q J 6 3
♣ 5 2

SOUTH
♠ 9 2
♡ A 9 3
◇ A
♣ A K Q J 9 7 4

NORTH	EAST	SOUTH	WEST
1 ♠¹	Pass	3 ♣²	Pass
4 ♠³	Pass	7 ♣⁴	Pass
Pass	Pass		

¹ Typical minimum Precision opener.
² With a self-sufficient club suit and definite slam interest, responder jump shifts to inform partner immediately that game is certain and slam likely.
³ Despite his 11 point opening, opener jumps to show the solid nature of his spade suit.
⁴ 13 tricks with clubs as trumps should be available, knowing that partner holds at least the AKQ10 x of spades which should cover all losers outside of trump.

This excellent grand slam was reached via a simple, direct auction with only 29 HCP in the combined hands! Effective slam auctions need not require Blackwood or hard-to-remember gadgets; they simply rely on the precise meaning of simple bids.

This concludes our discussion of major suit openings, responses, and subsequent rebids. Most of the principles we have been discussing are equally applicable when the auction begins with a Precision limited minor suit opening. However, it is important that you completely understand Precision's major suit openings before we consider the minor suit openings in Chapter 6. To aid your understanding, carefully consider all the questions in the following exercises and review any material you may have either forgotten or find confusing.

Exercise #3
Major suit openings, responses and rebids

What initial action would you take as the dealer with the following hands?

1. ♠ 10 8 5 3 2
♡ A K Q 10 5
◊ K 7
♣ 9

2. ♠ A K J 10 7
♡ K 6
◊ J 9 7 6 4 2
♣ –

3. ♠ K 7 6 3 2
♡ Q J
◊ K J
♣ J 8 7 4

4. ♠ A 10 9 7 6
♡ A Q 10 9 5
◊ 10 9 4
♣ –

5. ♠ A K J 10
♡ 9 6 4 3 2
◊ 8
♣ A 10 4

6. ♠ K Q J 5 2
♡ K Q
◊ A 10 9 3 2
♣ J

7. ♠ K Q
♡ 10 9 7 4 3
◊ A K Q J 10
♣ 6

Partner opens 1 ♡; what initial response would you make with the following hands:

8. ♠ A Q 7
♡ J 10 9
◊ A 10 9 3
♣ 8 7 4

9. ♠ 9 8 5 2
♡ K 10 4
◊ J 10 5 4
♣ A 6

10. ♠ A 4
♡ Q 10 9 6
◊ 3
♣ A K Q J 9 8

11. ♠ Q 10 7
♡ 10 9
◊ A Q 10 5
♣ K 10 9 6

12. ♠ J 10 9 3
♡ 8
◊ 9 8
♣ A Q J 6 3 2

13. ♠ 6 5
♡ K Q J 6
◊ Q J 10 7
♣ K J 5

14. ♠ 7
♡ K 10 6 5 2
◊ Q J 8 6 5 3
♣ 9

15. ♠ A K J 6 3
♡ 8
◊ A K J 10
♣ K J 10

16. ♠ K J 10
♡ J 10
◊ A Q 9 6
♣ Q J 10 9

Partner opens 1 ♠; what initial response would you make with the following hands:

17. ♠ 4 3
♡ A K Q 10
◊ Q 9 4
♣ J 10 5 4

18. ♠ 9 8
♡ J 10 5
◊ K 10 5 4 3 2
♣ Q 10

19. ♠ 10 9 6
♡ A 10 3 2
◊ K 9 4
♣ A 8 7

20. ♠ 7 6
    ♡ A 10 6 3 2
    ◇ 9
    ♣ A K J 9 6

21. ♠ J 10
    ♡ A J 9 3
    ◇ K 10 8 7
    ♣ K 9 2

What is your next bid in the following auctions:

OPENER	RESPONDER
1 ♡	1 ♠
?	

22. ♠ J 10 7
    ♡ K 10 9 4 2
    ◇ A Q 8
    ♣ K 10

23. ♠ 9 6
    ♡ A K 10 4 2
    ◇ A K J 10 5
    ♣ 5

24. ♠ K J 10 2
    ♡ A K 8 3 2
    ◇ K 10 4
    ♣ 8

OPENER	RESPONDER
1 ♡	1NT
?	

25. ♠ J
    ♡ A K J 3 2
    ◇ A 10 4
    ♣ 10 9 3 2

26. ♠ A 8 7
    ♡ A K J 10 7 6
    ◇ K 10 7
    ♣ 5

27. ♠ K J 10
    ♡ A 10 9 5 4
    ◇ K 9
    ♣ A 10 9

OPENER	RESPONDER
1 ♠	2 ♣
?	

28. ♠ Q 10 9 4 3
    ♡ K Q 10
    ◇ A Q 9
    ♣ 9 6

29. ♠ K Q 10 8 7
    ♡ A K J 10 4
    ◇ 7
    ♣ Q 10

30. ♠ K Q J 10 5
    ♡ K J 2
    ◇ A J 10
    ♣ 9 4

OPENER	RESPONDER
1 ♡	2NT
?	

31. ♠ K 10
    ♡ K J 10 9 3 2
    ◇ A Q 10
    ♣ J 10

32. ♠ A 10 3
    ♡ K Q 9 3 2
    ◇ Q 5 3
    ♣ 8 7

33. ♠ A 3
    ♡ J 10 9 5 3 2
    ◇ K Q J
    ♣ 9 8

	OPENER	RESPONDER
	1♠	3NT
	?	

34. ♠ K Q J 7 5
♡ K 3
◇ A J 10 5
♣ 6 5

35. ♠ A Q 10 4 3 2
♡ 7 4
◇ A Q 2
♣ J 2

36. ♠ A Q 9 8 3
♡ K 10 9 5 2
◇ Q 9
♣ 7

	OPENER	RESPONDER
	1♡	1♠
	2♣	?

37. ♠ K Q J 7
♡ 10 9
◇ A Q 4 2
♣ 8 7 3

38. ♠ A Q 10 9 4 2
♡ 10 9
◇ K 2
♣ Q 3 2

	OPENER	RESPONDER
	1♠	1NT
	2◇	?

39. ♠ 6 3
♡ J 10
◇ J 10 4
♣ A Q J 10 7 6

40. ♠ K 3
♡ A 9 8 2
◇ K 10 6 2
♣ 10 8 7

	OPENER	RESPONDER
	1♡	2♣
	3♡	?

41. ♠ K 10 2
♡ Q
◇ K 6 4 2
♣ A 10 9 4 2

42. ♠ A 6 4
♡ 4 3
◇ 7 4
♣ A K 10 9 6 2

	OPENER	RESPONDER
	1♠	2♡
	3♣	?

43. ♠ 7 5
♡ A K J 9 6 3
◇ K 4 2
♣ 3 2

44. ♠ 9 5
♡ A K Q 10 9 6
◇ A 4
♣ 9 8 4

	OPENER	RESPONDER
	1 ♠	3 ♣
	?	

45. ♠ K Q 10 5 2
  ♡ A J 2
  ◊ J 10 3 2
  ♣ J

46. ♠ A K Q J 7
  ♡ J 10 5
  ◊ 10 9 4
  ♣ 8 6

Answers
Exercise #3

1. 1 ♠
Do not be influenced by the relative strength of your two five-card suits. You should always open the higher ranking suit. Obviously, you intend to bid hearts next.

2. 1 ♠
Although we usually advise opening your six-card suit when you are six-five, this is a typical exception to that general rule. Holding a weak six-card minor and a strong five-card major it is best to open the major suit.

3. Pass
Despite our desire to "fire the first shot in the auction whenever possible," this 11 count does not merit opening. Seven of your puny 11 points are concentrated in your two doubletons and may be totally worthless. Both your long suits are weak and you lack defensive strength.

4. 1 ♠
Although we would not open #3 with its 11 HCP, we definitely would open the bidding with this fine 10 count. This exceptional 10 point hand contains 2½ quick tricks and the honors are concentrated in the two good five-card suits. The spot-cards are excellent and you have the additional advantage of a void. Your playing strength is far better than most hands containing 13 or 14 HCP.

5. 1 ♡
It is the length and rank of your suits, not their relative strength, which determines which suit you should open.

6. 1 ♣
You have 16 HCP, so you must open 1 ♣ playing Precision. Remember, first count your HCP and then consider your distribution and playing strength.

7. 1 ♡
No choice holding 5-5 distribution despite the weakness of the heart suit compared to the best five-card diamond suit you can hold.

8. 3 ♡
Perfect example of a Precision Limit Raise. Invitational, but not forcing. Three-card support headed by the jack-ten is sufficient since partner is known to have a five-card suit.

9. 2 ♡
No need to introduce your poor four-card spade suit with good three-card heart support. Limit your strength and show your support for partner's suit by making a simple raise to 2 ♡.

10. 3 ♣
Excellent illustration of a Precision jump shift. Prospects for slam are good. Alert partner immediately to your slam interest and then show your heart support.

11. 2NT
Perfect description of your balanced hand and scattered strength. Invitational, but NOT forcing. (Similar to a limit raise of partner's major in terms of strength: 11-13.)

12. 1♠
You cannot immediately introduce your fine six-card club suit in the auction since you lack the required 11 HCP for a two over one response. With only 8 HCP it is best to simply bid 1♠ over 1♡, hoping to introduce your club suit later in the auction.

13. 4♡
With 14 points in support of hearts you must force the bidding to game. Since you have no slam interest in light of partner's limited opening bid, simply conclude the auction by bidding game in hearts. Remember, there are two types of hands responder may hold when he raises directly to game after a 1♡ or 1♠ opening: (1) standard pre-emptive raise to four with long trump support, distributional values, and little defensive strength; or (2) a balanced opening bid lacking any slam interest.

14. 4♡
Typical example of a pre-emptive raise to game after a limited opening bid. Excellent support and distribution but little or no defensive strength. (Review the answer to #13).

15. 1♠
Although you have more than enough high-card strength to justify an immediate jump shift (20 HCP), it is best simply to respond 1♠ since you have no idea WHERE this hand should be played. Slam is extremely likely but careful probing is necessary to determine which slam to play.

16. 3NT
Describing your balanced game-going values with scattered strength. (Shows specifically 14-16 HCP and a doubleton in partner's suit.)

17. 2NT
Since you cannot bid 2♡ which would promise at least five hearts, the best description of your balanced 12 count with scattered strength is an invitational jump to 2NT.

18. Pass
Although 1♠ may not be the best final contract for your side, it is a playable one and you lack the values for any Precision response.

19. 3♠
Sound limit raise to 3♠ inviting partner to carry on to game with more than a minimum opening bid.

20. 2♡
With two five-card suits and sufficient values for a two over one response, always bid the higher ranking suit first, even if the lower ranking suit is stronger.

21. 2NT
Typical invitational jump to 2NT.

22. 1NT
Describing your 5-3-3-2 balanced minimum opening with scattered values.

23. 3♢
Typical Precision jump shift by a limited opener. Suggests at least 5-5 in the two suits bid as well as a maximum (14-15) in high cards.

24. 3♠
Invitational jump raise promising a good fit and a maximum 1♡ opening.

25. 2♣
Your hand is far better played in a suit than in notrump. Keep in mind that partner has denied holding either four spades or three hearts; therefore, your side must have a good fit in one, if not both, minor suits.

26. 3♡
Describing your maximum limited opener and fine six-card heart suit. Invitational but not forcing.

27. 2NT
If responder has a maximum 1NT response your side has reasonable chances to score a notrump game. You could not have a better hand and open 1♡. Excellent spot-cards for notrump.

28. 2NT
Best description of your 5-3-3-2 minimum with both unbid suits well stopped.

29. 3♡
Jump shift to show your excellent 5-5 and maximum limited opener.

30. 3NT
Partner has promised at least 11 HCP with his two over one response. 2NT would not be forcing and you certainly want to insist on reaching game after partner's initial re-

sponse.

31. 4 ♡
Since responder has shown 11-13 HCP and at least two hearts, your side has both sufficient assets for game and an eight-card heart fit. Remember, 3 ♡ would not be forcing.

32. Pass
Although 2NT is a forcing response using standard bidding methods, in Precision 2NT is simply invitational. So, with a minimum 11 count you should pass and hope partner can win eight tricks.

33. 3 ♡
In principle a sign-off promising a six-card suit.

34. Pass
Partner has shown 14-16 HCP with only two spades. Since you don't have an eight-card major suit fit and your hand is semibalanced, you should not consider bidding over 3NT.

35. 4 ♠
Knowing your side has an eight-card spade fit with sufficient values for game, you should "correct" 3NT to 4 ♠.

36. 4 ♡
Since partner holds only two spades and has promised a balanced hand he must have at least three hearts, giving you an eight-card (and possibly a nine-card) heart fit. "Correct" 3NT to your "known" heart fit.

37. 2NT
Invitational but NOT FORCING. Describes the same type of hand you might have jumped to 2NT directly, except that you hold four spades and wished to explore first for a possible major suit fit.

38. 3 ♠
Invitational but NOT forcing. Jump rebids by responder in a suit bid at the one-level describe a good six-card suit and approximately 11 or 12 points.

39. 3 ♣
You could not introduce your fine club suit immediately since you lacked the required strength for a two over one response. Having limited your strength by the initial 1NT response, you should now suggest your fine suit as a final contract.

40. 3 ◊
This hand is a sound raise of opener's second suit. Game is still possible, so you should not pass.

41. 3NT
Opener has shown a maximum limited opening with a good six-card heart suit, making game a virtual certainty. It is best to show your game-going values and stoppers in the unbid suits by bidding the no-trump game.

42. 4 ♡
Your side has both adequate strength for game and an eight-card heart fit. 4-3 is sufficient support for partner's good six-card suit.

43. 3 ♡
Although you have a diamond stopper, repeat your hearts with a six-card suit and a relative minimum two over one response. Opener should be in a good position to determine the best final contract.

44. 4 ♡
With both a self-sufficient trump suit and game-going values, you should jump directly to game in your suit. Remember, 3 ♡ would not be 100% forcing and you certainly don't want this deal passed out short of game.

45. 3NT
As we advised in the text, it is not a good idea to introduce a weak second suit after partner jump shifts. With scattered values and no fit for partner's suit, a simple no-trump rebid is best.

46. 4 ♠
This is the exact hand C. C. Wei held, as discussed in the text. A jump rebid in opener's suit shows a solid suit (no worse than AKQ10x).

Chapter 7

Minor Suit Openings

PRECISION MINOR SUIT openings are automatically limited by three factors we have already discussed.

(1) *Your failure to open 1 ♣ limits your high card strength to less than 16.*

(2) *Since you would open an intermediate notrump with a balanced 13-15 point hand, your hand is either unbalanced or you hold an 11 or 12 count.*

(3) *With the rare exceptions of 6-5 or 7-5 distribution, it is most unlikely that you have a five-card major since you did not open 1 ♡ or 1 ♠.*

These three factors should enable you to bid as easily and accurately over Precision's minor suit openings as you can over either 1 ♡ or 1 ♠.

The 2 ♣ opening bid

Suppose you are the dealer and pick up:

♠ K 10 7   ♡ 8   ♢ K 5 3   ♣ A Q J 10 6 2

You canot open 1 ♣ since that bid is reserved for all strong hands. Therefore, you must open 2 ♣ playing Precision.

Two clubs is a natural bid, showing a *good* club suit and 11-15 HCP. Opening 2 ♣ suggests you have either a six-card club suit or a five-card suit plus a four-card major. The reason why most 2 ♣ openings fall into one of these categories is that when four diamonds and five clubs are held, it is often best to open 1 ◊; and when the distribution is 5-3-3-2 with scattered strength, or if the five-card club suit is weak, 1NT or 1 ◊ is preferred.

Let's consider a few examples:

(a) ♠ Q 10 5   ♡ K 9   ◊ A J 10   ♣ K 10 7 3 2

Holding a relatively weak five-card club suit with scattered strength and balanced distribution, it is best to open 1NT on this 13 count.

(b) ♠ 10 9 5 3 2   ♡ A 5   ◊ 6   ♣ A K Q J 10

You must open 1 ♠ not 2 ♣. Remember, with 5-5 distribution always open the higher ranking suit, irrespective of their relative strength.

(c) ♠ 7 5   ♡ A K J 7   ◊ 4   ♣ K 8 6 4 3 2

Although your club suit is rather poor, you do have six of them and the values for a limited opening bid. Since you cannot open 1 ♡ (holding only four), 2 ♣ is your choice.

(d) ♠ Q J   ♡ Q J 2   ◊ Q 5   ♣ K 8 7 5 3 2

Despite the 11 HCP, this hand does not qualify for a limited Precision opener. You have no defensive strength and the quality of your points could hardly be worse.

(e) ♠ K 4   ♡ 8 5   ◊ A K J 3   ♣ Q J 8 5 3

It is better to open 1 ◊ rather than 2 ♣ when you are 4-5 in minors and the club suit is not exceptional.

(f) ♠ A 10 9 4   ♡ 6   ◊ A K 4   ♣ Q 9 6 3 2

Here again, the objection to opening 2 ♣ is the weakness of the suit. Since 1NT is out of the question in light of the singleton heart, we advise opening 1 ◊. (As we shall discuss later in this chapter, opening 1 ◊ does not promise any particular length or strength in diamonds.)

(g) ♠ 7   ♡ A Q 10 5   ◊ 6 5   ♣ K Q J 10 9 4

A perfect 2 ♣ opening – a fine club suit coupled with a good four-card major.

Remember, the key to the Precision 2 ♣ opening is the quality of the club suit. Do not open 2 ♣ unless your suit is good. If you hold the values for a limited opening bid with a relatively poor club suit, consider opening 1NT or 1 ◇.

Responding to 2 ♣

Since opener's strength and distribution are clearly defined by his 2 ♣ opening, responder's task is quite simple. By using the Limited Bid Strategy he is usually able to determine immediately whether game is out of reach, possible, or should be bid. With an exceptionally fine responding hand the same holds true for slam.

The following box outlines the recommended responding structure:

	Over 2 ♣	
Responses:	**Meaning and Development**	**HCP:**
Pass	No interest in game.	0-7
2♡, 2♠	Five-card or longer suit; invitational, but NOT forcing. The opener may then: (a) Pass with a minimum if the contract is playable. (b) RAISE with interest in game and a fit. (c) BID 2NT with a maximum and scattered strength. (Implies semi-balanced distribution.) (d) Correct the contract to 3 ♣ or bid 2 ♠ over 2 ♡ if partner's suit is not playable.	8-10
2NT	Balanced hand inviting game in notrump. No interest in the majors. The opener may then: (a) PASS with a minimum and a semi-balanced hand playable in notrump. (b) RAISE to 3NT with a maximum playable in notrump. (c) Bid 3 ♣ with a minimum or jump to 4 ♣ with a maximum that will play better in in a suit. (Responder is expected to pass	11-13

3♣ but is invited to carry 4♣ on to 5♣.)

3♣	Constructive raise, invitational but NOT forcing. xxx is adequate support.	8-10
4♣	Pre-emptive raise, with good trumps. (High card strength depends on distribution and vulnerability.)	4-7
3◇, 3♡, or 3♠	Good five-card or longer suit, game forcing, and may have slam interest. The opener may then: (a) RAISE responder's suit with a fit. (b) BID 3NT with some scattered strength in the unbid suits, lacking a fit for partner's suit. (c) BID a NEW SUIT to show a concentration of values, inviting responder to bid 3NT with the unbid suit stopped. (d) REBID his club suit with no attractive alternative call.	14-up
3NT	Sign-off with scattered strength and sufficient assets for game using the Limited Bid Strategy.	14-16
2◇	Conventional FORCING response. Does not promise any length or strength in diamonds; it simply asks opener to tell more about his hand. The opener answers as follows: *With a Minimum Opening Bid (11-13 HCP)* 2♡ = four-card heart suit. 2♠ = four-card spade suit. 2NT = no four-card major, relatively balanced hand with scattered outside strength. 3♣ = no four-card major, unbalanced hand, six or more clubs. *With a Maximum Opening Bid (14-15 HCP)* 3♡ = four-card heart suit.	11-up

3 ♠ = four-card spade suit.
3NT = no four-card major, relatively balanced hand with either scattered
strength or a source of tricks via a
fine club suit.
4 ♣ = no four-card major, highly unbalanced hand unsuitable for notrump, six or more clubs.
Given this precise information regarding
opener's hand, responder is usually able to
set the final contract.

The conventional 2 ◊ response should be used on all good hands
where the eventual contract is in considerable doubt. It is often a better
choice than jumping in a relatively weak five-card suit with game-going
values. Remember, opener's rebid over 2 ◊ will not only clarify the
nature of his distribution but define his point count as well.

Let's look at a few examples (partner opens 2 ♣ and you hold):

(a) ♠ J 10 9 5 3   ♡ K 6 3 2   ◊ K 7   ♣ 10 9

PASS. Game is out of reach. Partner has promised a good club suit so
2 ♣ should be a reasonable contract.

(b) ♠ 9 8 5   ♡ 10 9   ◊ A K Q 10 5   ♣ 10 8 7

3 ♣. You cannot bid your good diamond suit since 2 ◊ would be conventional showing 11 or more HCP saying nothing about diamonds and 3 ◊
would be game-forcing promising the values of a sound opening bid.
Therefore, make a constructive raise of opener's suit. xxx is more than
adequate support for partner's known good suit.

(c) ♠ K Q J 9 4 2   ♡ A 10 7   ◊ K 5   ♣ J 4

3 ♠. Forcing to game showing a reasonable five-card or longer suit.
Remember, 2 ♠ would not be forcing, and you certainly want to drive
the bidding to game with this fine hand.

(d) ♠ A Q 7   ♡ Q 10 9   ◊ Q 10 9 3 2   ♣ J 8

2NT. Inviting partner to carry on to game with more than a minimum 2 ♣ opener. 2NT denies four cards in either major since you would have used the 2 ◇ inquiry with interest in either major suit.

(e) ♠ K 10 9 7 3   ♡ A Q J 5   ◇ A 4   ♣ J 6

2 ◇. Although you have ample strength and the required five-card suit to jump to 3 ♠, it is best to begin your search for the optimum final contract with 2 ◇. 2 ◇ will locate a fit in either major suit immediately and tell you a great deal about partner's opener. You can always bid 3 ♠ (forcing except over 2 ♠) next if partner's rebid denies a four-card major.

(f) ♠ K 5   ♡ A Q J 10 4   ◇ 9 7 6 5   ♣ 5 4

2 ♡. Invitational but not forcing. Game is possible if partner holds either a maximum 2 ♣ opener or a good fit for hearts.

(g) ♠ 9 8 2   ♡ Q 4   ◇ K Q 10 9 6 3   ♣ 8 7

PASS. Since you cannot bid 2 ◇ naturally, you should pass.

(h) ♠ 6   ♡ 5 3   ◇ Q J 10 5 4 2   ♣ K 8 7 5

4 ♣. Pre-emptive jump raise. The enemy must have an excellent fit in one if not both majors. With favorable vulnerability, you might even jump to 5 ♣.

(i) ♠ 6   ♡ A K Q 10 5 3 2   ◇ 9 8   ♣ J 7 6

4 ♡. Bid what you think you can make. With your club fit, game in hearts should be an excellent proposition. You may also block your opponents out of a good spade or diamond contract.

(j) ♠ K J 10 5   ♡ K Q 10 3   ◇ A 10 3   ♣ 10 9

2 ◇. Explore for a major suit fit before settling in a notrump game.

(k) ♠ K J 10   ♡ A Q 5   ◇ Q J 10 3   ♣ J 8 7

3NT. No interest in the majors and sufficient assets for game; jump directly to 3NT with your scattered 14 count and balanced distribution.

The Precision 2 ♣ opening describes in one bid a hand that frequently takes two or three bids to describe using standard bidding methods. Since, playing Standard American, you are often forced to open 1 ♣ with a relatively worthless club holding, you may have to rebid a good club suit two or three times to inform partner you hold both a real suit and a minimum opening bid. Playing Precision this is accomplished in one bid, and you have the added advantage of limiting your overall strength and distributional possibilities.

A 2 ♣ opening may also pre-empt your opponents when the hand actually belongs to them. It is far more dangerous to compete at the two-level with marginal values than it is at the one-level. And opener's partner is in an excellent position to judge both sides' potential should the auction become competitive. Several successful penalty doubles have taken place after an opening 2 ♣ bid when an opponent has entered the bidding on doubtful values and found his partner with a worthless dummy. During the 1976 Summer National Team Game Championship a 2 ♣ opening egged a former world champion into a disastrous overcall that tipped the scales in favor of the Precision Team in a close, hard-fought match.

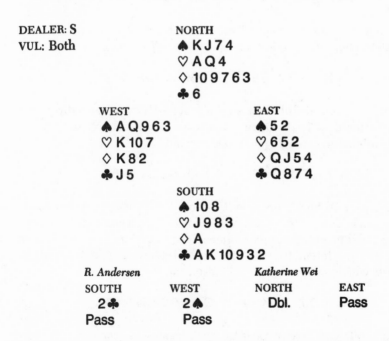

DEALER: S
VUL: Both

NORTH
♠ K J 7 4
♡ A Q 4
♢ 10 9 7 6 3
♣ 6

WEST
♠ A Q 9 6 3
♡ K 10 7
♢ K 8 2
♣ J 5

EAST
♠ 5 2
♡ 6 5 2
♢ Q J 5 4
♣ Q 8 7 4

SOUTH
♠ 10 8
♡ J 9 8 3
♢ A
♣ A K 10 9 3 2

R. Andersen		*Katherine Wei*	
SOUTH	WEST	NORTH	EAST
2♣	2♠	Dbl.	Pass
Pass	Pass		

RESULT: Down 5: N-S + 1400

Certainly the punishment (−1400) was a bit unfair for West's crime of overcalling 2 ♠ with the values for an opening bid and a reasonable five-card suit. As West sadly noted in the postmortem, exchange the North and East hands and his side would have been cold for a spade game and very likely would never have gotten in the bidding had he passed! We cannot argue with that analysis. It does, however, illustrate an additional advantage of Precision's 2 ♣ opening.

The versatile 1 ◇ opening

The Precision 1 ◇ opening bid shows 11-15 HCP but does not promise any length or strength in diamonds. Like the "short club" opening bid favored by standard bidders who do not open four-card majors, the Precision 1 ◇ opening is used with hands that clearly merit an opening bid but which don't meet the requirements for any of the other Precision openings. This takes care of those hands that do not contain a five-card major and are unsuitable for 1NT or 2 ♣ openings. For example:

(a) ♠ K Q 10 4   ♡ 6   ◇ A J 7   ♣ Q 7 5 4 2

Open 1 ◇. You cannot open 2 ♣ with such a weak club suit and your singleton heart disqualifies the hand for a 1NT opening.

(b) ♠ K J   ♡ A Q 5   ◇ Q 7 6   ♣ 10 8 7 5 3

Open 1 ◇. Your distribution is suitable for a 1NT opening but you lack the required 13 HCP. Open 1 ◇ intending to rebid 1NT to describe your minimum (11 or 12 point) opening bid.

(c) ♠ 7   ♡ J 10 4 3   ◇ A K Q 10 6 5   ♣ 8 4

Open 1 ◇. Although opening 1 ◇ does not promise any length or strength in diamonds, it does NOT deny holding a good diamond suit. Your hand meets all the requirements for a Precision limited opening bid, and you intend to rebid your fine suit unless partner responds in hearts which, of course, you will raise.

(d) ♠ A Q 7   ♡ K 10   ◇ Q 9 8 5 2   ♣ K 10 4

Open 1NT. Best description of this semi-balanced 14 count with scattered strength and a relatively weak diamond suit.

Although the range for a Precision 1 ◊ opening is 11-15 HCP (like other Precision limited openings), the minimum strength cannot be defined strictly in terms of high card points. Since 1 ◊ can be opened on several distributional possibilities, the quality of your points, distribution, defensive strength, overall playing strength, and possible rebids are all factors to be considered in determining whether to open a marginal hand with 1 ◊. Our general rule of thumb is to open all 12 point hands that do not qualify for any other Precision opening with 1 ◊.

As for opening 11-point hand with 1 ◊, we suggest *not* opening when you:

(1) *Hold 4-3-3-3 distribution.*
(2) *Hold 4-4-3-2 distribution without either major suit.*
(3) *Whenever partner's response might not allow us a simple, descriptive rebid.*

Consequently, we would open 1 ◊ with:

(a) ♠ A 10 9 4   ♡ A K 9 8   ◊ 10 9 7 5   ♣ 4
(b) ♠ 6   ♡ K Q 10 9   ◊ A Q 10 9 5   ♣ 10 9 7
(c) ♠ A 10 9   ♡ A 10 8 7   ◊ Q J 10 9 3   ♣ 3
(d) ♠ 3   ♡ A 9 8 5   ◊ A K 10 7 4   ♣ 9 8 2

Note that in all the examples your honors are working together in your long suits, and frequently you are blessed with good working spot cards which often mean a trick or two in the play. Rebids would rarely be a problem with any of these hands no matter what partner responds. And should partner double the opponents in a competitive auction, all four hands have reasonable defensive strength. Contrast (a) − (d), which we would open, with the following hands which also contain 11 HCP that we do *not* recommend opening:

(e) ♠ Q J   ♡ K Q J   ◊ Q 8 7 4 3   ♣ 8 7 5
(f) ♠ A 4   ♡ A 5 2   ◊ Q J   ♣ 8 7 6 5 3 2
(g) ♠ K J   ♡ Q J 4   ◊ Q J 3 2   ♣ J 7 5 2

To produce game opposite any of these hands responder would practically have to hold a 1 ♣ opener.

You will recall that we advocate opening more 11-point hands when you have a five-card major or a good club or diamond suit. Opening 1 ◊ with balanced and semi-balanced 11 count that are not exceptional is generally a losing tactic. Precision will get you into the bidding often enough, so that when it comes to opening marginal hands with 1 ◇ you should follow the basic safety law in passing another automobile on the highway: "When in doubt, DON'T."

Responding to 1 ◇

As with the other Precision limited openers, the first rule in responding to 1 ◇ is to pass with a bad hand. The normal minimum for a response at the one level is 8 HCP. It may be tempting to respond with less when you are short in diamonds, since the opener may also be short, but such temptations should be resisted. In practice, 1 ◇ is rarely passed out and even if it is, there is no law that partner can't have four or five diamonds. Remember, constructive bidding becomes impossible if the early bids are not soundly based.

Your first obligation in responding to 1 ◇ is to explore for a possible major suit fit. So that 4-4 fits in a major suit will not be lost, responder should introduce any four-card major over an opening 1 ◇. Even with a longer minor and the vaues to make a two over one, responder should first show a four-card major. Although this is contrary to standard practice when responder holds a good hand, playing Precision it works out best for two reasons:

(1) It insures your side will never miss establishing an eight-card or longer fit in either major, even if the auction becomes highly competitive.

(2) It gives the opener an economical opportunity to describe the nature of his 1 ◇ opening. This is particularly important considering the broad range of hands that must be opened 1 ◇, playing Precision.

Consequently, we would respond 1 ♠ after partner's 1 ◇ opening on either:

(a) ♠ K J 10 4   ♡ A 5   ◇ J 10   ♣ A Q J 10 4

or

(b) ♠ Q 8 7 5   ♡ 6   ◇ K 8   ♣ A K 10 7 4 3

Raising partner's 1 ◇ opening is similar to raising 1 ♡ or 1 ♠ in terms of the strength shown. However, you must have far better trump support since 1 ◇ does not promise any particular length or strength in diamonds. *A minimum of five-card support is required for all raises.* The following table outlines the Precision requirements for raising a 1 ◊ opener:

After a 1 ◊ opener		
Responder bids:	**Description**	**Supporting Points:**
2 ◊	At least five-card support; denies a four-card major.	8-10
3 ◊	At least good five-card support (Q10xxx or better). Suggests an unbalanced hand (unsuitable for notrump); Denies a four-card major.	11-13
4 ◊ or 5 ◊	Pre-emptive raise with good, long trump support and little outside high card strength (at least six-card support and usually seven.) High Card strength depends on distribution and vulnerability.	No specific range

Notrump responses to a 1 ◊ opening follow the exact ranges of bidding notrump over a 1 ♡ or 1 ♠ opening. Needless to say, all notrump responses deny holding four cards in either major suit. For your convenience and review, the following table outlines the Precision notrump steps over 1 ◊:

Over 1 ◊		
Responder bids:	**Description and Development:**	**HCP:**
1NT	Suggests a balanced hand with neither a four-card major nor good five-card diamond support.	8-10
2NT	INVITATIONAL, but NOT forcing. Promises a balanced hand with scattered strength. Denies four hearts or spades. Must include diamond strength.	11-13
3NT	Balanced hand with scattered strength. No four-card major.	14-16

Often it is better to make a notrump response with a semi-balanced hand including five relatively weak diamonds rather than make a constructive raise. For example, we would bid 1NT over 1 ◊ holding:

(a) ♠ A Q   ♡ Q 10 5   ◊ J 9 6 4 2   ♣ J 10 7

and would jump to 2NT rather than bid 3 ◊ with:

(b) ♠ K 10   ♡ K Q 10   ◊ Q 10 4 3 2   ♣ Q 8 7

This is because it is easier to make a nine trick game at notrump than eleven tricks at diamonds.

Jump shifting over 1 ◊ denotes the same types of hands which you would need to jump shift over either 1 ♡ or 1 ♠. Responder must have a self-sufficient suit, good controls, and more than moderate interest in slam. It is never a good idea to jump shift with two or three suited hands, since you can rarely afford the bidding space consumed. This is particularly true over 1 ◊ due to the broad range of hands covered by this opening bid.

The "Bidding Rule of 11" applies to responding 2 ♣ over 1 ◊. Remember, no matter how good or long your suit is, you cannot directly introduce a suit at the two-level without 11 HCP. And since responder's first obligation is to explore for a possible major suit fit, the opener can presume that responder does not hold four cards in either major when responds 2 ♣.

This principle of bidding a four-card major first (even with a long club suit or exceptional fit for diamonds) has important consequences on the second round of bidding. Suppose you open 1 ◊ holding:

♠ A J 10 3   ♡ K J 9 5   ◊ K 10 4   ♣ 9 8

Partner responds 2 ♣. There is no reason to introduce either major since partner has denied holding four cards in either suit. Rebid 2NT describing your balanced minimum with scattered strength not strong enough for a 1NT opening.

The precision 2 ◊ opening bid

Suppose you are the dealer and pick up:

(a) ♠ A Q 7 4   ♡ K Q 10 5   ◊ 7   ♣ K 10 8 7

(b) ♠ A K 10 3   ♡ A Q 10 6   ◊ −   ♣ 9 8 5 3 2
(c) ♠ K 10 9 5   ♡ A K J   ◊ J   ♣ J 5 4 3 2

All of these sound limited opening bids would be opened 1♣ using standard bidding methods. Needless to day, that opening call is not available to Precision partnerships on these hands because they do not include 16 HCP. Since you cannot open one of a major without a five-card suit and must have a balanced hand to open 1NT, by the process of elimination you would be forced to open 1◊, not a very appetizing choice. In order to avoid opening 1◊ when you hold a singleton or even void in diamonds, the Precision 2◊ bid was devised. But it has other far-reaching advantages.

The Precision 2◊ opening bid shows 11-15 HCP and 4-4-1-4, 4-4-0-5 (with a weak club suit), 4-3-1-5 or 3-4-1-5 (with a weak club suit) distribution pinpointing shortness in diamonds. Although you are bidding diamonds, you are really showing the other three suits simultaneously. (Thus, this 2◊ opening bid is similar in concept to the "Unusual Positive" discussed in Chapter 2.)

Since the 2◊ opening covers a wide range of hands it is important that you have tools available to clarify the opener's holding. As the following box suggests, the key to clarification is the 2NT response.

Opening 2◊
(11-15 HCP, short in diamonds, 4-4-1-4; 4-4-0-5; 4-3-1-5; 3-4-1-5.)

Responses:	Description and Developments:
Pass	At least six diamonds; no fit for any of opener's suits.
2♡, 2♠, 3♣	Sign-off
2NT	Asks for distribution, and Opener rebids: 3♣ = 3-4-1-5 distribution. 3◊ = 4-3-1-5 distribution. 3♡ = 4-4-1-4 distribution with min. (11-13) 3♠ = 4-4-1-4 distribution with max. (14-15) 3NT = 4-4-1-4 distribution with singleton ace or king of diamonds with maximum. 4♣ = 4-4-0-5 and minimum. 4◊ = 4-4-0-5 and maximum.

Note: All subsequent diamond rebids by responder ask for controls* — e.g.

2 ◇ - 2NT
3 ♡ - 4 ◇ = asks for controls
1st step = 0-2
2nd step = 3
3rd step = 4 (etc.)

(Over a 4 ◇ rebid by opener, 4NT asks for controls.)
*An ace = 2 controls
A king = 1 control

When partner opens 2 ◇ and the Limited Bid Strategy shows that game is out of reach, your primary objective as responder is to find a playable part-score contract. With three potential trump suits that partner has suggested, you can sign off by bidding 2 ♡, 2 ♠, or 3 ♣. On rare occasions you may pass 2 ◇ if you have six or more diamonds with no fit for any of partner's suits. (You'll need at least six diamonds since partner has no more than one and may be void.) Let's consider a few examples: Partner's 2 ◇ opening is passed to you holding:

(a) ♠ Q J 3 2   ♡ 5 4   ◇ K Q 10 9 5   ♣ 9 7

BID 2 ♠. Game is out of reach and your side should have a reasonable play for 2 ♠. You should not consider passing 2 ◇ which can be at best a 5-1 fit.

(b) ♠ A Q 10 5   ♡ K J 10 3   ◇ 9 7 3   ♣ 10 9

BID 2NT. Game is possible if opener has more than a minimum 2 ◇ opening. Remember, partner will pass either 2 ♡ or 2 ♠, and in the event opener has 4-3-1-5 or 3-4-1-5 distribution you might very well miss your 4-4 fit and play a 4-3 fit.

(c) ♠ 6 3 2   ♡ 5   ◇ Q J 10 7 6 4   ♣ K 9 6

Pass. 2 ◇ is likely to be your best contract on this misfit part-score deal.

When responder has a good fit for one of the suits shown by opener's 2 ◇ bid and game is possible, he should make an invitational jump to

3 ♡, 3 ♠, or 4 ♣. These jumps are not forcing but urge the opener to carry on to game with more than a minimum 2 ◇ opening. Jump to 3 ♡ over a 2 ◇ opening holding either:

(a) ♠ A 5 2   ♡ K Q 10 4 2   ◇ 7 5 4   ♣ J 10

or

(b) ♠ 6 5   ♡ A J 10 9 5   ◇ 9 8 4   ♣ A J 6

If responder sees chances for game and needs further information about partner's hand, 2NT is the best response. Opener's rebid will clearly define his hand both in terms of strength and distribution. For example:

(a) ♠ K J 10 7   ♡ A Q 10 5   ◇ 6 4 2   ♣ K 3

Bid 2NT over 2 ◇ to determine your side's best final contract. You have a 4-4 fit in at least one of the majors and slam is not out of the question if opener has a maximum with a void in diamonds.

(b) ♠ K 10 4 2   ♡ Q J   ◇ A Q 10 9 5   ♣ J 10

Bid 2NT over 2 ◇ intending to sign-off in 4 ♠ if partner's rebid shows that he holds four spades or in 3NT if partner has 3-4-1-5 distribution.

If you have 11-13 HCP and a very good six-card or longer diamond suit, invite game in notrump by "raising" to 3 ◇. And if your six or seven card diamond suit is solid with an outside entry, you may simply jump to 3NT over 2 ◇. (It is best to have an outside card as a potential entry in the event that partner is void in diamonds. Without an outside card, you might elect to bid 2NT and then rebid 3NT having discovered that partner has one diamond.)

All jumps to game are sign-offs. Opener is expected to pass.

Should your opponents compete after your side has opened 2 ◇, responder is usually in an excellent position to judge what action is best for your side. If your opponents have made an error by competing, responder should not hesitate to double them, knowing a great deal about opener's hand. All other bids should be natural following the general principles outlined in the box, with the obvious inference that responder is bidding freely. 2NT over an enemy overcall or double of 2 ◇ should be conventional as it is in a non-competitive auction.

Exercise #4
Minor suit openings, responses, and rebids

What initial action would you take as the dealer with the following hands:

1. ♠ A Q 10 7
♡ K 6
◊ A J 10 9 5 3
♣ 8

2. ♠ 10 9 5 3 2
♡ A K
◊ K Q J 10 9
♣ 3

3. ♠ A K 10
♡ K Q 9
◊ 8 7
♣ 9 8 5 3 2

4. ♠ A Q J
♡ K 10
◊ Q 9 8 6 4
♣ K 10 3

5. ♠ 7 4
♡ J 10
◊ A K 10 5
♣ K J 10 9 3

6. ♠ K J 10 6
♡ A Q 10 5
◊ 6
♣ K J 7 5

7. ♠ A J 10 3
♡ 6
◊ A K
♣ J 9 8 5 4 2

8. ♠ 3
♡ K Q J 10
◊ 6 4
♣ A J 10 9 5 3

9. ♠ —
♡ A Q 10 5 2
◊ A K 10 7 4 3
♣ Q J

10. ♠ A J 10 7
♡ K Q 10 5
◊ 6 5
♣ Q 10 4

Partner opens 2 ♣; what initial response would you make holding:

11. ♠ K 10 9 4
♡ A Q 10 2
◊ A 9 8
♣ J 10

12. ♠ 9 8 2
♡ A Q 10 9 3 2
◊ J 10
♣ Q 7

13. ♠ Q J 10
♡ A Q 6
◊ Q 10 7 5
♣ 8 7 4

14. ♠ J 9 7 4 3 2
♡ J 10 5
◊ Q 10
♣ J 10

15. ♠ 9 5
♡ A Q J 10 9
◊ A J 10 2
♣ Q 7

16. ♠ 4
♡ 8 7
◊ A 7 5 4 3 2
♣ Q 8 4 2

Having opened 2 ♣, what rebid would you make in the following auctions:

OPENER	RESPONDER
2 ♣	2 ◊
?	

17. ♠ 1 0 9 4 2
♡ A 3
◇ 6
♣ A K J 9 4 2

18. ♠ J 1 0 4
♡ K 1 0
◇ Q 1 0
♣ A K 9 8 5 2

19. ♠ K Q 1 0 5
♡ 6
◇ K 3
♣ A Q J 7 5 4

20. ♠ A 3 2
♡ 5
◇ J 1 0 2
♣ K Q J 1 0 4 2

Partner opens 1 ◇, what initial response would you make holding:

21. ♠ 8 5 2
♡ J 1 0 4 2
◇ A K J 6 3
♣ 9

22. ♠ A Q
♡ K 1 0 2
◇ Q 4 3 2
♣ J 1 0 5 4

23. ♠ 1 0 9 6 5
♡ 4
◇ K 1 0 5
♣ A K Q J 6

24. ♠ A J 4
♡ 7
◇ K Q 8 7 4 2
♣ J 1 0 2

25. ♠ J 6 5
♡ Q J
◇ J 1 0 4 2
♣ J 1 0 9 5

Partner opens 2 ◇, what initial response would you make holding:

26. ♠ 5
♡ A 1 0 9
◇ Q J 1 0 7 4
♣ 1 0 9 6 3

27. ♠ Q 1 0 7
♡ K 6
◇ K Q J 9 5
♣ A 1 0 6

28. ♠ A J 9 5
♡ Q 8 4
◇ A J 1 0 5 3
♣ Q

29. ♠ A 1 0 9 5 2
♡ J 1 0
◇ 8 7 5 3
♣ K 4

30. ♠ K Q 1 0 3
♡ 7 6 3
◇ K Q 4
♣ J 3 2

Answers
Exercise #4

1. 1 ◇
It's legal to have a good diamond suit when you open 1 ◇.

2. 1 ♠
Although you have a fine five-card diamond suit and five bad spades, always open your higher ranking suit with 5-5 distribution.

3. 1 ◇
Never open 2 ♣ with a weak five-card suit. It is better to open 1 ◇ on your doubleton since you lack the strength for 1NT.

4. 1NT
Good description of your balanced 15 count with scattered strength.

5. 1 ◇
Although your club suit is not particularly weak, it is still best when you have four good diamonds with five clubs to open 1 ◇.

6. 2 ◇
A perfect Precision 2 ◇ opening.

7. 1 ◇
You cannot open 2 ♣ with such a poor suit; 1 ♠ would promise a five-card suit and you can't open 1NT with such unbalanced distribution even though you have the required strength. Open 1 ◇, it is your only choice.

8. 2 ♣
Your club suit is good enough to open 2 ♣. If partner bids 2 ◇ you'll show your fine four-card heart suit next.

9. 1 ♣
You have 16 HCP.

10. 1 ◇
You have full values for a Precision limited opener but are a point short of an intermediate notrump opening.

11. 2 ◇
Explore for a possible 4-4 major suit fit. If partner' doesn't have a four-card major, sign-off in 3NT.

12. 2 ♡
Non-forcing. If opener "corrects" the contract to 3 ♣ you should pass.

13. 2NT
Invitational, but not forcing. Suggesting a balanced hand, 11-13 HCP, without a four-card major.

14. Pass
Despite your six-card suit, you should not consider bidding 2 ♠ with such a weak hand. 2 ♣ is playable with your good doubleton.

15. 3 ♡
Forcing to game promising at least a good five-card suit.

16. 4 ♣
Pre-emptive raise. Your opponents must have a good fit in one of the majors (if not both). Make it difficult for them to get together. At favorable vulnerability you might even bid 5 ♣.

17. 2 ♠
Do not be concerned about the weakness of your four-card spade suit. Partner didn't ask you whether you had a good four-card major, only if you have a four-card major.

18. 2NT
Describing your minimum semi-balanced 2 ♣ opening with scattered strength.

19. 3 ♠
Showing a maximum 2 ♣ opener with four spades.

20. 3 ♣
Informing partner you have a minimum 2 ♣ opener without a four-card major.

21. 1 ♡
Your first obligation is to bid a four-card major if you have one. If opener doesn't raise hearts you intend to support diamonds.

22. 2NT
Perfect description of your balanced 12 count with scattered strength. Invitational but not forcing. Denies a four-card major.

23. 1 ♠
Do not be tempted by your excellent club suit to by-pass your weak four-card spade

suit. Remember your first responsibility over 1 ◇.

24. 3 ◇

A jump to 3 ◇ describes 11-13 points in support of diamonds, usually with good six-card support. Similar to jump-raising 1 ♡ or 1 ♠ except you need much better and longer trump support since opener may be short.

25. Pass

Playing Standard American you probably would be forced to respond. No reason to respond playing Precision since opener's hand is limited.

26. 3 ♣

Play your 4-4 or 4-5 club fit.

27. 3NT

Bid what you think you can make. You have sufficient values for game without an eight-card major suit fit and diamonds well-stopped despite partner's shortness.

28. 2NT

If opener has four spades you intend to sign-off in 4 ♠, but if partner is 3-4-1-5 then 3NT should be your side's best game contract. Bid 2NT and find out.

29. 3 ♠

Despite your limited high card strength, this hand has great playing strength when partner opens 2 ◇. You have no wastage in diamonds; five trumps, and the jack of hearts and king of clubs should be very useful. Invite partner to bid 4 ♠ with more than a minimum 2 ◇ opening.

30. 2 ♠

We advised inviting game on (29) with an eight count, but on this 11 count we would not consider a move toward game. The diamond strength is wasted facing a singleton or void and our 4-3-3-3 distribution is undesirable. Any move in the direction of game might carry your side too high.

Chapter 8

When Your Opponents Compete Over 1 ♣ or 1NT

FOR SOME TIME there was a popular belief that strong club systems could be disrupted by direct competition. "Suppose over 1 ♣ the next player bids 2 ♠," the theory ran, "Then the Precision partners have to start exchanging information at the three-level."

This myth has been destroyed by most experienced Precision partnerships. The reason is simple. Your 1 ♣ opening, promising 16 or more high card points, gives your side at least as good a basis for handling highly competitive auctions as a nebulous one bid in standard bidding systems. In addition, competition adds tools to your responding arsenal that you do not have in non-competitive auctions, particularly the penalty double when your opponents attempt to fight cannons with water pistols!

Consequently, you should not fear competition over a 1 ♣ opening; you should welcome it. Exploit your opponent's interference either by making a penalty double (when they have plunged beyond their depth) or by using their bid(s) to assist you in determining your side's best contract. In order to do this, you must make only a few adjustments in your responding structure and develop firm partnership understandings as to what various bids mean in competitive auctions, especially which bids are forcing and which are not.

Responses over a takeout double

If the opponents make a takeout double of the 1 ♣ opening bid, no bidding room has been lost. The double is in no way obstructive; on the contrary, it provides responder with two additional calls — pass and redouble. By using these two additional bids, responder can make his initial response even more precise, adopting the following structure:

		After a Double of 1 ♣
Response:	**HCP:**	**Meaning:**
Pass	0-4	Minimum negative response; any distribution
Redouble	8-up	Positive response; forcing to game; suit(s) unknown
1 ◇	5-7	Maximum negative response; tends to be balanced since responder could bid a reasonable five-card suit.
1 ♡, 1 ♠ 2 ♣, 2 ◇	5-7	Non-forcing; shows a five-card suit that you would have bid after making a negative 1 ◇ response had 1 ♣ been passed.
2 ♡, 2 ♠ 3 ♣, 3 ◇	8-up	Unusual Positive response. Usual meaning.
1NT	8-10	
2NT	11-13	Usual meaning; balanced hands.
3NT	14-15	

As this table outlines, both the positive notrump responses and the Unusual Positive responses remain the same. The positive suit responses are handled by redoubling, which gives your side an opportunity to make a penalty double if your opponents err by bidding one of your suits. And the negative 1 ◇ response you would have given without the intervening double is now clearly defined into three categories:

(a) Minimum negative (0-4 HCP): Pass
(b) Maximum balanced negative (5-7 HCP): 1 ◇
(c) Maximum unbalanced negative (5-7 HCP): 1 ♡, 1 ♠, 2 ♣, 2 ◇ (showing a five-card suit)

Using these methods an enemy takeout double of 1 ♣ actually enhances your ability to exchange information. Let's consider a few examples. Suppose partner's 1 ♣ opener is doubled on your right. With each of the following examples, what action would you take?

(1)   ♠ Q 10 7   ♡ A J 9   ◇ 9 8 4 3 2   ♣ K 6

Bid 1NT. The response you would have made had right-hand opponent passed. Remember, notrump responses are not affected by your opponent's double.

(2) ♠ J 10 5 3 2   ♡ 6 5 2   ◊ 9   ♣ 9 7 6 3

Pass. Warn partner immediately that you hold a pitiful hand.

(3) ♠ Q J 10 4   ♡ A 10 5 3   ◊ K 8 7 5   ♣ 6

Bid 3 ♣. Make the Unusual Positive response you would have made in a non-competitive auction.

(4) ♠ K J 10 7 3   ♡ 8   ◊ J 10 4 2   ♣ 10 9 5

Bid 1 ♠. You would have been forced to bid 1 ◊ without the double, but now you can show your good five-card suit with only 5 to 7 HCP.

(5) ♠ A 8 4   ♡ Q J 10 8 3   ◊ J 10 7   ♣ 8

Redouble. You cannot bid 1 ♡ directly since that would deny the values for the positive response which you have. A redouble will show that you have 8 or more HCP; later you can bid your suit. (Who knows, perhaps your opponents will bid hearts presenting you with an excellent penalty double.) And, knowing that you hold 8 HCP or more partner may be able to double a suit bid by your left-hand opponent.

(6) ♠ J 10 6   ♡ 8 4   ◊ K Q J 10 5 2   ♣ 4 3

Bid 2 ◊. You cannot bid 1 ◊ since that would indicate a balanced 6 or 7 point hand (maximum negative) and say nothing about diamonds. Jump to 2 ◊ to show that you have a maximum negative response plus a good diamond suit.

After partner's initial response (positive or negative) over the takeout double, all rebids by opener are natural and carry their non-competitive meaning. If responder's initial response was positive (redouble, notrump, or an Unusual Positive), the partnership is forced to game. If the partner of the takeout doubler bids a suit, a double by opener is for penalties, and a cue bid shows a strong three-suited hand with a singleton or void in the enemy suit.

Except for the additional bids available to both responder and opener, this approach to handling takeout doubles over a 1 ♣ opening requires very few changes from your non-competitive 1 ♣ auctions. In fact, the enemy double should make your bidding even more precise.

Handling overcalls of 1 ♣

Unlike a takeout double, an enemy overcall of 1 ♣ does consume bidding space. Therefore, it is necessary to make a few adjustments in your responding structure. We recommend the following structure:

After an Overcall of 1 ♣		
Response:	**HCP:**	**Meaning:**
Pass	0-7	Negative response. If in the upper range (5-7), responder does not have a good five-card or longer suit.
Double	8-up	Positive response.
New Suit	5-7	Five-card or longer suit that responder would have bid after making a negative 1 ◊ response in a non-competitive auction.
Jump in a Suit	8-up	The Unusual Positive response with shortness in the suit bid.
Notrump	8-10 11-13 14-15	Usual meaning; balanced hand with stopper(s) in the enemy suit. (A simple NT bid denotes 8-10, a jump in notrump shows 11-13, and a double jump in notrump describes 14-15.)
Cue-bid	11-up	Definite slam interest with at least second round control in the enemy suit.

After responder's initial action over an opponent's overcall, all rebids by opener are natural and convey their usual meaning. Obviously, no-trump rebids promise stopper(s) in the enemy suit in addition to a balanced hand. If the response was positive (double, the Unusual Positive, notrump, or a cue-bid), the partnership is forced to game. Therefore, jump bids in a suit indicate the quality of the suit and do not promise additional HCP.

When your opponents drive the bidding immediately to the two, three, or even four-level, use essentially the same methods advised over simple overcalls. The higher the level, the better hand you must have to enter the bidding. Although we would bid 1 ♠ after a 1 ♡ overcall of partner's 1 ♣ opening holding:

♠ K J 7 3 2   ♡ 6 3   ◊ J 10 3 2   ♣ 7 5

we would not bid 3 ♠ over a jump to 3 ♡. 3 ♠ would not be forcing but could lead to a disaster if the deal is a misfit and opener has a poor fit for spades.

After high level interference bids, doubles by both responder and opener tend to be more cooperative in nature based more on general strength than simply a good holding in the enemy suit.

This completes our discussion of handling competition over 1 ♣. As in all aspects of contract bridge, there is no substitute for reason and judgment. Do not be pushed into foolish bids at high levels because your opponents compete. Such action is often very costly and can have serious consequences on partnership confidence and morale. In short, always have the values your bids imply. And be prepared to double erring opponents who attempt to fight cannons with pea-shooters.

Exercise #5
Handling competition over 1 ♣

What initial response would you make in the following auctions?

	OPENER	OPPONENT	RESPONDER
	1 ♣	Dbl.	?

1. ♠ Q J 8 5
   ♡ K 5
   ◊ 8 6 5 2
   ♣ 9 8 6

2. ♠ A J 10 5 2
   ♡ 8 7 3
   ◊ J 10 5
   ♣ 8 4

3. ♠ K J 10 4
   ♡ A 10 6 5
   ◊ Q 7 6 2
   ♣ 3

4. ♠ K J 10
   ♡ A Q 10 7 6
   ◊ 7 6
   ♣ 8 4 3

5. ♠ Q 9 8 5 3 2
   ♡ 7 6 2
   ◊ 4
   ♣ 10 9 3

6. ♠ K 10 4
   ♡ K 7
   ◊ Q 10 4 2
   ♣ J 10 5 3

	OPENER	OPPONENT	RESPONDER
	1 ♣	1 ♠	?

7. ♠ 7 5
   ♡ A Q 10 6 3
   ◊ K 10 7 4
   ♣ 9 5

8. ♠ A Q J
   ♡ J 10 7
   ◊ K 10 4 3
   ♣ 9 8 3

9. ♠ 7
   ♡ 8 7 4
   ◊ A Q J 10 7
   ♣ 9 6 4 3

OPENER	OPPONENT	RESPONDER
1♣	2♠	?

10. ♠ 5 4
♡ K Q 10 9
◇ A J 7
♣ 9 8 5 3

11. ♠ 7
♡ K J 10 8 7 3
◇ J 10 4 2
♣ 9 8

Answers
Exercise #5

1. 1◇
Showing a maximum negative response (5-7 HCP) and suggesting a reasonably balanced hand since you would have bid a good five-card suit.

2. 1♠
Showing a five-card suit that you would have bid after making an initial 1◇ (negative) response had 1♣ been passed.

3. 3♣
The Unusual Positive response describing your 4-4-4-1 distribution with 8 or more HCP.

4. Redbl.
You cannot bid 1♡ directly since that would deny the values for a positive response. Redouble and then bid your heart suit.

5. Pass
Warn partner immediately that you hold a very poor hand (0-4 HCP).

6. 1NT
Although you have the values for a redouble, it is best to describe this balanced nine count by making a positive (8-10 HCP) 1NT response.

7. Dbl.
2♡ would not be forcing and would deny the values for a positive response. Double first (showing a positive response) and then bid your good five-card suit.

8. 2NT
Describing a balanced 11 to 13 point hand with spades well-stopped.

9. 2◇
Showing your good five-card suit and a hand that does not meet the requirements for a positive response.

10. Dbl.
Showing a positive response.

11. 3♡
Invitational, but not forcing. Shows a good suit without the values for a positive response. (Tends to be a fairly good suit and hand at this level, just short of a positive response.)

When the enemy competes over 1NT

You should not fear competition over a 13-15 point 1NT opening; you should welcome it! Competition gives you a chance to add the penalty double to your arsenal of responses.

The penalty double is particularly useful against those players who react to weak or intermediate notrump openings in much the same fashion that charging bulls respond to waving red flags. Somehow, their hands always seem to get better, or they assume partner must have great values because the opener does not have 16 or 17 high card points. Remember, when partner opens an intermediate 1NT responder is as well-placed to double an overcall as when the opening bid is considered a strong notrump. When an opponent makes an error in judgment by competing on marginal values or when his trump suit is breaking badly, punish him!

When your hand is not suited for a penalty double after an enemy overcall, you have the following choices:

(1) PASS. The hand belongs to the enemy and your hand does not justify any form of competition.

(2) MAKE A NON-FORCING, SIMPLE SUIT RESPONSE. Any non-jump in a new suit over an overcall simply says you wish to compete but have no interest in game. (Except for 3 ♣ which we use as the Stayman Convention in all competitive auctions.) For example:

	OPENER	OPPONENT	RESPONDER	
(a)	1NT	2♡	2♠, or 3♢	=Five-card or longer suit; Non-forcing.
(b)	1NT	2♣	2♢, 2♡, 2♠	=Five-card or longer suit; Non-forcing.
(c)	1NT	2♢	3♣	=The Stayman Convention asking for a four-card major.

(3) MAKE AN INVITATIONAL RAISE TO 2NT. Same meaning as a non-competitive raise to 2NT (10 or 11 points).

(4) MAKE A FORCING RESPONSE, choosing any of the following:

(a) Jump in a new suit below the game level, e.g.:

OPENER	OPPONENT	RESPONDER	
1NT	2♡	3♠, 4♣, 4♢	=FORCING

(b) Bid 3♣ — The Stayman Convention. Opener responds:

3♢: No four-card major and no stopper in the enemy suit.

3♡: Four-card heart suit; may also have four spades.

3♠: Four-card spade suit; denies four hearts.

3NT: No four-card major; promises stopper in the enemy suit.

(c) Cue bid the enemy suit. This promises at least game-going values and asks opener to bid 3NT with a stopper in the opponent's suit.

Lacking a stopper, opener should suggest a trump suit. Cue-bids are 100% forcing to game and may be the start of a slam investigation.

(5) JUMP TO GAME OR SLAM. Sign-offs, carrying their usual meaning.

If your partner's opening 1NT bid is greeted by a penalty double, it is important that you have methods to handle the following situations:

(1) You wish to escape from 1NT doubled when you have either (a) a weak one-suited hand or (b) a weak hand that contains no long suit but will undoubtedly play better in a suit than 1NT, including 4-4-4-1 hands.

(2) You wish to inform partner immediately that your side has the balance of strength and that you are happy to play 1NT doubled, or to double the opponents should they elect to run.

If a 1NT opening is doubled, use the following structure:

After a Double of 1NT	
Bid:	**Meaning:**
Redouble	8 or more High Card Points. ("We have the balance of strength.")
2♣	The Stayman Convention. (Less than 8 HCP)
2◇, 2♡ 2♠, 3♣	Weak, one-suited hand. (Less than 8 HCP)
Pass	Less than 8 HCP suggesting that responder has no five-card or longer suit and requesting opener to "rescue" himself in his lowest ranking four-card suit. Does NOT imply a desire to play 1NT doubled.

If you are presently using other methods after your opponents have competed over 1NT, and these have proved effective, continue using them. Our goal is simply that you establish understandings, so that your partnership can easily distinguish bids which are strong from actions which are not.

Using the methods outlined, let us consider a few examples:

(1)	OPENER	OPPONENT	RESPONDER
	1NT	2♡	?

(a) ♠ K Q 10 7 5   ♡ 6   ◇ A J 10 3   ♣ K 7 6

Bid 3 ♠. You cannot bid only 2 ♠ since a simple suit response would be non-forcing and you hold game-going values. You must force opener to bid by jumping. Although 3 ♣ (the Stayman Convention) would ask partner if he held four spades, three-card support is all you need.

(b) ♠ A 10 7   ♡ Q 10 8 2   ◊ Q J 10 3   ♣ J 10

Double 2 ♡. Although you have the values to invite game by bidding 2NT, the penalty at 2 ♡ is likely to be considerable with your opponents holding no more than seven trumps in their combined hands and little or no strength in the dummy.

(c) ♠ A J 10 5   ♡ A 3   ◊ K 10 5 3 2   ♣ 10 8

Bid 3 ♣ (the Stayman Convention). You intend to bid 3NT if partner does not have four spades, but you should explore for a possible eight-card major suit fit before settling in 3NT.

(2)	OPENER	OPPONENT	RESPONDER
	1NT	2 ◊	?

(a) ♠ K J 10 6 3 2   ♡ A Q 2   ◊ 8 5   ♣ Q 10

Bid 4 ♠, the same call you would have made in a non-competitive auction. Your side has a minimum of eight spades and you have the values for game.

(b) ♠ 8   ♡ Q 10 9 3 2   ◊ J 10 4 2   ♣ 10 9 3

Pass. Although you would have bid 2 ♡ had your opponents remained silent (an effort to improve the contract in light of your singleton spade), you have been relieved of that task by the overcall. Your best hope for a plus score is to let the opponents play 2 ◊.

(c) ♠ A K 3   ♡ J 10 4   ◊ 7   ♣ A Q J 9 7 3

Cue-bid 3 ◊. You have game-going values without any real interest in the major suits, which eliminates Stayman from consideration. Partner's first obligation in responding to a cue-bid is to bid 3NT with a guard in the enemy suit, which you will pass since nine tricks should be available. If partner fails to bid 3NT, 5 ♣ should be a reasonable undertaking.

(3)	OPENER	OPPONENT	RESPONDER
	1NT	Double	?

(a) ♠ J 10 6 3 2   ♡ 2   ◊ J 10 8 3   ♣ 7 4 3

Bid 2♠. It is unlikely you will make it, but it should play considerably better than 1NT. At least your hand will produce a trick or two at spades, which is more than it is likely to produce at notrump.

(b) ♠ Q J 10   ♡ K Q 8 7 4   ◇ J 10 5   ♣ 9 8

Redouble. Alert your partner immediately that your side has the balance of strength. (Remember, a redouble simply says you have 8 or more HCP and all other bids deny holding as much as an eight count.)

Let us turn to some quiz examples to see if you have mastered the principles we have discussed.

Exercise #6
Handling competition over 1NT

As responder, what action would you take in the following auctions?

OPENER	OPPONENT	RESPONDER
1NT	2♡	?

1. ♠ A 8 5
    ♡ K 3
    ◇ Q J 10 5 2
    ♣ J 7 4

2. ♠ K Q J 8 3
    ♡ 4
    ◇ A J 10 3
    ♣ K 5 2

3. ♠ Q J 10 5
    ♡ A 2
    ◇ K J 10 4
    ♣ Q 9 7

4. ♠ A 4
    ♡ Q 10 8 3
    ◇ K 5
    ♣ 10 9 8 5 2

5. ♠ K J 10 6 3
    ♡ 5
    ◇ K 8 5
    ♣ 9 8 3 2

6. ♠ A 6 2
    ♡ 4
    ◇ A K Q 10 9 5
    ♣ J 10 8

OPENER	OPPONENT	RESPONDER
1NT	Dbl.	?

7. ♠ K J 10 2
    ♡ Q 7 5
    ◇ J 10 4 3
    ♣ J 10

8. ♠ 10 9 8 4
    ♡ Q J 8 6
    ◇ J 10 9 3
    ♣ 7

9. ♠ 8
    ♡ 3 2
    ◇ J 10 9
    ♣ K J 10 9 6 5 2

10. ♠ 8 7 5 2
     ♡ Q 10
     ◇ J 10 7 4
     ♣ 10 9 3

Answers
Exercise #6

1. 2NT
Invitational. Although you have sufficient strength for a penalty double, holding only a doubleton trump and a good offensive hand it is best to invite game.

2. 3♠
Forcing to game; describes a good five-card suit.

3. 3♣
The Stayman Convention. Remember, after a two-level overcall, 3♣ is NOT natural; it asks opener to bid an unbid four-card major. With this hand, you will raise to game if partner bids 3♠ or bid 3NT if he bids 3♢.

4. Double
An ideal penalty double of an enemy overcall. Your opponents have no more than seven trumps and you can expect a lucrative set on a part-score deal.

5. 2♠
Not forcing, but constructive in the sense that you are not simply "correcting" 1NT to a better contract. With a very poor hand you could simply pass 2♢.

6. 3♡
Excellent hand for a cue-bid asking opener to bid 3NT if he has the enemy suit stopped. If partner fails to bid 3NT, 5♢ should be a reasonable undertaking.

7. Redouble
Promises eight or more HCP, informs opener that your side has the balance of strength and invites partner to double any enemy "escape" effort.

8. 2♣
The Stayman Convention, hoping to escape from 1NT doubled into a playable suit contract.

9. 3♣
Describes your weak, one-suited hand. 2♣ would be Stayman, and with 8 or more HCP you would redouble.

10. Pass
Less than 8 HCP; suggests that responder has no long suit and requests opener to "rescue" himself in his *lowest* ranking four-card suit. Does not imply a desire to play 1NT doubled.

Chapter 9

Other Competitive Auctions

SINCE THE "FLOOR" of Precision's limited openers is considerably lower than in most other bidding systems, you should anticipate a high percentage of competitive auctions when you don't open 1♣. When you open many 11 and most 12 point hands, you must be prepared for aggressive competition. This chapter is designed to guide you to the best result in contested auctions.

Competitive auctions rarely create serious problems for Precision partnerships for two reasons:

(1) You need adopt very few changes in the meaning of both initial responses and rebids. (However, you can profit by establishing understandings for bids unavailable to you in non-competitive auctions: for example: redoubles, doubles, cue-bids, etc.)

(2) Responder has the immediate advantage of knowing the limit of opener's high card strength (less than 16) and a great deal about his distribution. (This is particularly useful when the enemy jumps directly to a high level.)

Often you will be able to make good use of your opponent's bidding both in the auction and subsequently in the play.

If an opponent makes a takeout double of a limited opening bid, no bidding room has been lost. The double is in no way obstructive; on the contrary, it both pinpoints enemy strength (implying support for the unbid suits, particularly majors) and gives responder an additional weapon — the redouble.

Consequently, partnerships need make *no* changes in their responding structure. ALL responses and rebids convey their non-competitive meaning after a takeout double. Simply ignore the double and respond naturally. This approach has the advantage that neither partner will forget a modified or specialized response, and the saved memory work is energy that can be applied to the play.

However, over takeout doubles, there is no reason not to add the redouble to your arsenal. It can be a deadly weapon when your side has the balance of strength and the deal is a misfit. Our recommended requirements for a REDOUBLE are:

(1) 10 or more HCP

(2) No exceptional fit for opener's suit

(3) Interest in penalizing the opponents (even at a low level)

Obviously, you are not forced to redouble simply because you have 10 or more HCP. Let's consider a few examples:

(1)	OPENER	RHO	YOU
	1 ♡	Dbl.	?

Responder holds:

(a) ♠ K J 10 9 2   ♡ 5   ◇ A Q 4   ♣ Q 10 9 3

REDOUBLE. You may collect a huge set on a deal when your side cannot score even a game. On defense your singleton heart may be a great asset, not a liability. You should double anything your opponents bid. (LHO's hand must qualify for federal assistance as a disaster area!) Alert partner immediately to your excellent defensive prospects, and warn him against rebidding his suit.

(b) ♠ 5   ♡ K Q 9 3   ◇ A K 4 2   ♣ J 10 5 3

BID 3 ♠. With such an excellent fit for hearts you should not consider doubling your opponents at a low level. Make the bid you would have made in a non-competitive auction − a splinter-bid (double jump), describing a strong raise of opener's suit with shortness in the bid suit.

(c) ♠ A 5   ♡ 10 9   ◇ 5 4 2   ♣ A Q J 10 7 5

BID 2 ♣. With no interest in doubling two of the three unbid suits (and it is rather unlikely your opponents will bid clubs), make your natural two-over-one response promising 11 HCP.

After a redouble, any new suit introduced by the redoubler is forcing for one round. So are jump raises of any suit bid by opener. Simple notrump bids or non-jump raises of a suit bid by opener are invitational. Remember, the "floor" of a redouble is 10 HCP but the "ceiling" is unlimited. For example:

(1)	OPENER	OPPONENT	RESPONDER	OPPONENT
	1 ◇	Dbl.	Redbl.	1 ♡
	Pass	Pass	1NT	
			NOT FORCING	

Responder must hold a balanced 10 or 11 point hand with a heart stopper but insufficient length or strength in hearts to make a double desirable.

(2)	OPENER	OPPONENT	RESPONDER	OPPONENT
	1 ♡	Dbl.	Redbl.	1 ♠
	Pass	Pass	2 ♣	
			FORCING	

Responder must have a club suit and is unable to double 1 ♠. Opener must not pass.

(3)	OPENER	OPPONENT	RESPONDER	OPPONENT
	1 ◊	Dbl.	Redbl.	Pass
	Pass	1 ♡	Pass	
			FORCING	

A cue-bid by responder who has previously redoubled forces the bidding at least to game and asks opener to further describe his hand. Let's say the bidding goes:

	OPENER	OPPONENT	RESPONDER	OPPONENT
	1 ♡	Dbl.	Redbl.	1 ♠
	Pass	Pass	?	

and responder holds:

♠ A 3 2   ♡ Q J   ◊ K J 10 6   ♣ K 7 5 4

Cue-bid 2 ♠. It is difficult to judge what the best game contract for your side is without knowing more about opener's hand. 3NT, 4 ♡, or even 5 ♣ or 5 ◊ are all possible. Use the cue-bid to explore the possibilities.

The opener has an opportunity to add the redouble to his arsenal when responder's initial response is doubled. Although less "penalty-oriented," it can be a valuable tool in describing opener's hand. Use a redouble by *opener* to describe:

(a) A maximum limited opener.
(b) At least a partial fit for responder's suit (if his response was not notrump).
(c) Good defensive strength as well as offensive potential.

Following the policy of disregarding opponents' takeout doubles, all other rebids convey their non-competitive meaning, except that opener may pass the takeout double with no convenient rebid and a minimum opening hand. For example:

	OPENER	OPPONENT	RESPONDER	OPPONENT
	1 ♠	Pass	2 ♣	Dbl.
	?			

(a) ♠ A Q 10 9 2   ♡ A Q 10   ◊ K 10 5   ♣ 10 9

REDOUBLE. You have a maximum 1 ♠ opener and good defensive values located behind the enemy strength. Inform partner immediately that you have a good hand. Doubling a low-level contract may be your side's best result, particularly if partner is short in spades.

(b)   ♠ K Q J 3 2   ♡ A   ◇ 10 9 4   ♣ Q 5 4 2

RAISE to 3 ♣. Show your excellent club fit for partner just as you would have done in a non-competitive auction.

(c)   ♠ A K 10 7 6   ♡ A 8 7   ◇ 9 8 4   ♣ J 10

PASS. You are no longer forced to bid, and you have nothing more to say about this minimum opening.

(d)   ♠ A Q J 10 9 5   ♡ A K 4   ◇ 7 5   ♣ J 8

JUMP to 3 ♠. Don't let your opponent's double stop you from describing your maximum opening and semi-solid six-card suit.

By bidding naturally over your opponents' takeout doubles and adding the redouble to your responding and rebidding arsenal, your auctions should be as precise over takeout doubles as they are in non-competitive auctions.

After an enemy overcall

Your initial response to partner's limited opening may be affected by an opponent's overcall. The bidding space consumed by the overcall may deny you the opportunity to make the response you would have made in a non-competitive auction. You cannot bid 1 ♡ over 1 ◇ should your opponent overcall 1 ♠, nor can you use the conventional 2 ◇ response over 2 ♣ if there is a 2 ♠ overcall. However, with a few adjustments you can handle overcalls as easily as takeout doubles. And immediately you can add the penalty double as a weapon when an opponent makes a bid that is not going to work out well for his side. You will find that having the opening bid strictly limited in high card strength and clearly defined distributionally is most helpful over all forms of enemy competition, particularly overcalls.

In general, we advise *no* changes in the meaning of raises, new suits introduced, and notrump responses after an overcall. All responses and rebids convey their non-competitive implications. Any bid that would be forcing in a non-competitive auction is forcing in a competitive auction. The same is true of invitational or non-forcing calls. The key is keeping in mind the level at which the bid is made. For example:

(1)	OPENER	OPPONENT	RESPONDER
	1 ◇	1 ♡	1 ♠

The 1 ♠ response promises 8 or more points and at least four spades as it would in a non-competitive auction. But,

	1 ◇	1 ♠	2 ♡

would promise 11 points and imply a five-card heart suit. The reason is simple. Responder has introduced a new suit at the two-level so the "Bidding Rule of 11" applies. Whereas it takes only 8 HCP to introduce a suit at the one-level, it takes 11 to bid a new suit at the two-level. The same is true if the auction goes:

	1 ◇	2 ♣	2 ♠
			11 or more HCP

(2)	OPENER	OPPONENT	RESPONDER
	1 ♡	1 ♠	3 ♡

Responder has 11-13 points in support of hearts. The same would be true if the bidding went:

	1 ♠	2 ♣	3 ♠
			11-13 & spade fit

or

	1 ◇	1 ♡	3 ◇
			11-13 & diamond fit

Notrump responses and rebids after an overcall are exactly the same (keeping in mind the level) as they would be in a non-competitive auction. Obviously, bidding notrump after an overcall does promise a stopper in the enemy suit. Should the bidding go:

	OPENER	OPPONENT	RESPONDER
	1 ◇	1 ♠	1NT

responder should have 8-10 HCP, balanced distribution, and a spade stopper. Either jumping to 2NT or bidding 2NT over a two-level overcall describes 11-13 HCP, balanced distribution, and the opponent's suit securely stopped. 3NT would show a balanced 14-16 HCP and stoppers.

Jump shifts (and splinter-bids over major suit openings) are not affected by overcalls.

In addition to jump shifts, one other vehicle is available to describe a powerful hand when your opponents overcall a limited opening bid — a CUE-BID in the enemy suit. Let's say you pick up:

♠ 5   ♡ A K Q 10   ◇ A Q 10 5   ♣ K Q J 7

or

♠ A   ♡ K Q 10 9   ◇ K J 10 9   ♣ A K 10 7

and the bidding starts:

OPENER	OPPONENT	YOU
1 ◇	1 ♠	?

BID 2 ♠. Although with either hand you have ample strength for a jump shift, you don't have a suit to jump in. The solution is to cue-bid your opponent's suit. A direct cue-bid describes the following:

    (a) A powerful hand with slam interest;

    (b) Control in the enemy suit (usually shortness);

    (c) No good, *long* suit to suggest as trump via a jump shift.

Now, let's turn our attention to our favorite bid after an overcall — the penalty double.

The penalty double

There are three important features in your hand you should look for when you are considering a double of an overcall of partner's opening bid:

(In order of importance)

    (1) Shortness in partner's suit

    (2) Strength in high cards — usually at least a good 9 HCP or better

    (3) Length and strength in the enemy suit.

Although all three are important, you will note that your holding in their suit is the least important of the three. The reason is simple. The most profitable penalty doubles take place when the deal is a misfit. When you don't have a fit for partner's suit, the less you are likely to make by playing the hand, and correspondingly, the more you are likely to profit from doubling your opponents. You need some general defensive strength (2), since partner should feel free to double your opponents should they attempt to escape from the contract you have doubled. Needless to say, when you have (1) and (2), the longer and stronger your trump holding is the greater the penalty is likely to be.

In addition to the hand you hold, there are three other factors to consider in doubling an overcall:
  (a) The vulnerability
  (b) What your side is likely to make by playing the hand versus what you are likely to collect by doubling. (Is there any danger they might make the contract and the game if you double?)
  (c) Your opponents and partner.

Doubling an overcall is similar to an investment. "How much do you stand to gain?" versus "How much do you stand to lose?" coupled with "What is the likely result of alternative courses of action?" The vulnerability is often the key to answering these questions. Obviously, the most desirable situation is when the opponents are vulnerable and you are not. Although you should never double for a one-trick set (there are far too many things that can go wrong in making such close doubles), even a two trick set against non-vulnerable opponents is very little compensation for a vulnerable game. Your potential loss from a penalty double is greatly increased if the double allows the opponents to score a game. For example, if there are no part-score considerations, there is far less risk in doubling 2 ♣ or 2 ◊ than in doubling 2 ♡. At worst, your opponents will only score a part-score, not a game.

There is also a human element to consider in doubling a part-score. Bridge players are creatures of habit. If the player who overcalls is known to be very conservative (the type who usually has an extra ace for his bids), do not double unless your hand is ideally suited for a penalty double. On the other hand, if you are playing against a highly competitive opponent who bids with the slightest excuse, we tend to double more aggressively.

A double of an overcall is most effectively played as a strong *suggestion*, not a command. It should be a cooperative venture, not a unilateral decision that cannot be overruled. Unfortunately, some players consider "pulling" partner's double as equivalent to "trumping partner's ace." Playing with such partners it is best to have an ideal hand before you double. There is also an old rubber bridge maxim that is worth recalling, particularly after your opponents have scored a doubled contract: "If your opponents never make a doubled contract against you, you're not doubling often enough!"

Let's consider a few examples:

(1)	OPENER	OPPONENT	RESPONDER
	1 ◊	1 ♠	?

Both sides vulnerable, no part-score considerations. Responder holds:

(a) ♠ K J 10   ♡ Q J 10   ◊ K 7 2   ♣ K Q 10 5

Although a penalty double of 1 ♠ might work out very well, we would jump to 3NT. Your spade holding will be as useful on offense as on defense. Prospects for a vulnerable game are excellent; bid the notrump game as you would in a non-competitive auction.

(b) ♠ Q J 10 8 6   ♡ A 5 2   ◊ 9   ♣ A 9 8 4 3

DOUBLE 1 ♠. Your opponent has made a serious blunder; you may collect a huge set on a deal where your side cannot score a game. This deal may be a complete misfit for both sides.

(2)   OPENER   OPPONENT   RESPONDER
           1 ♠   2 ◊   ?

You are not vulnerable against vulnerable opponents, no part-score considerations. Responder holds:

(a) ♠ A Q J 5   ♡ 9   ◊ K 9 8 3   ♣ 9 8 4 2

BID 3 ♠. Far too much of your strength and length is in partner's suit to double 2 ◊. Besides, your opponents may have an excellent heart fit. Make the constructive (invitational, but not forcing) jump-raise you would have made in a non-competitive auction.

(b) ♠ 9 3   ♡ 7 6   ◊ K J 10 9 6 3   ♣ 10 4 2

PASS. Yes, you are a prohibitive favorite to beat 2 ◊, but that is the only contract you rate to beat. If you double 2 ◊ and partner doubles their "escape," your position would be hopeless. Remember, you must have some general defensive strength to double an overcall.

(c) ♠ —   ♡ A 10 5 2   ◊ Q 9 6 3 2   ♣ A 9 8 3

DOUBLE. An ideal penalty double of 2 ◊. Your opponents are vulnerable and 2 ◊ is likely to be a holocaust. You have *no* fit for spades (somewhat of an understatement) and the ability to double any "escape."

Since the double of an overcall is a strong suggestion, not a command, let's examine a couple of auctions from the opener's vantage point.

(1)   OPENER   OPPONENT   RESPONDER   OPPONENT
           1 ♠   2 ♣   Dbl.   Pass
            ?

Opener holds:

(a) ♠ A K Q 10 7   ♡ A 10 3   ◊ 9 8 4 2   ♣ 10

PASS. You should be delighted to defend 2 ♣ doubled. Partner is very likely to be extremely short in spades. Do not consider rebidding your fine five-card spade suit; it will probably take several tricks on defense against 2 ♣. Your hand can hardly be a disappointment to partner.

(b) ♠ Q J 9 7 6 2   ♡ A Q J 10 7   ◇ Q 10   ♣ –

BID 2 ♡ or, if you feel aggressive, jump to 3 ♡. Your hand is far better offensively than it is defensively. Partner may have a fine fit for your good five-card heart suit. Also, you lack a trump to lead through declarer in case it is important to remove dummy's trumps.

(2)	OPENER	OPPONENT	RESPONDER	OPPONENT
	1 ♡	2 ♣	Dbl.	2 ◇
	?			

Opener holds:

(a) ♠ A J 2   ♡ A 10 9 3 2   ◇ A J 9   ♣ 8 7

DOUBLE. You have excellent defensive strength against any contract. Partner has implied he is short in hearts which suggests the deal is a complete misfit. If 2 ◇ doubled becomes the final contract, plan to lead the ace of hearts and continue hearts with your quick re-entries in both trump and spades.

(b) ♠ A 10 9 2   ♡ A K 6 5 3 2   ◇ J 10   ♣ J

PASS. You would have passed 2 ♣ doubled had it been passed by your right-hand opponent. Pass 2 ◇ around to partner and see if he can double.

Over jump overcalls and pre-emptive tactics

When the opponents pre-empt the auction immediately with a jump overcall, no simple guides or principles will permit you always to make the decision leading to your side's optimum result. At bridge, there is no substitute for reason and judgment. In practice, we attempt to follow the counsel of the great British expert, S. J. Simon, whose philosophy was "Get the best result possible; not necessarily the best possible result." We have found that this is good advice in resolving just about all bridge problems.

In addition to good judgment (which is most important), the key to handling pre-emptive tactics and jump overcalls (whether they are weak, intermediate or strong) is firm partnership understanding as to what competitive bids mean at high levels. This is particularly vital in terms of which bids are forcing and which are not.

In general, we advise very few changes in the meaning of raises, new suits introduced, and notrump responses after the enemy jumps the bidding, keeping in mind the level at which the bid is made.

OPENER	OPPONENT	RESPONDER
1 ♡	2 ♠	3 ♣

Obviously, 3 ♣ in this auction is not a strong jump shift. However, since it is a new suit, it is 100% forcing and suggests a minimum of a good 11 count.

OPENER	OPPONENT	RESPONDER	OPPONENT
1 ♠	3 ♣	3 ♠	Pass
?			

A jump overcall to 3 ♣ over partner's 1 ♠ opening prohibits partner from giving a simple 2 ♠ raise or an invitational jump raise in your suit. If responder bids 3 ♠ over 3 ♣ the question arises, is 3 ♠ a simple raise (8-10 points) or an invitational raise (similar to jumping to 3 ♠ over 1 ♠ showing 11-13 points in support of opener's suit)? We believe the best answer is a combination of both. 3 ♠ in this position should describe a "floor" of an exceptional simple raise (9+ or usually 10 HCP) to a "ceiling" of a good limit jump raise 11 or 12 points in support). If responder has a maximum limit jump raise (13 points) we suggest that he "bite the bullet," committing the hand to game by bidding 4 ♠. Therefore, with a near minimum: opener should pass.

Let's consider a few examples:

(1)	OPENER	OPPONENT	RESPONDER
	1 ♡	2 ♠	?

Responder holds:

(a) ♠ 5 3 ♡ Q 10 9 2 ◇ A J 10 5 ♣ Q 10 9

BID 3 ♡. Had your right-hand opponent passed, you would have bid only 2 ♡. But you do have a maximum simple raise with excellent spot-cards and good four-card trump support.

(b) ♠ J 6 ♡ 9 8 5 ◇ K J 6 5 ♣ Q J 9 3

PASS. Although you would have raised 1 ♡ to 2 ♡ in a non-competitive auction, you are far too weak to raise to 3 ♡ competitively.

(c)   ♠ A Q   ♡ J 10   ◇ K 10 4 2   ♣ J 9 8 5 2

BID 2NT. Invitational, showing the values for a non-competitive (and non-forcing) jump to 2NT over 1 ♡ with spades stopped.

(d)   ♠ Q J 9 4   ♡ 8   ◇ A 5 4 3 2   ♣ K 10 7

DOUBLE. Your hand meets all the requirements for a penalty double. You are short in partner's suit, have reasonable high card strength, and a good trump holding.

(2)	OPENER	OPPONENT	RESPONDER
	1 ◇	2 ♡	?

Responder holds:

(a)   ♠ K 10 2   ♡ K J 3   ◇ J 10 4   ♣ A Q 10 9

BID 3NT. Remember, 2NT would not be forcing. You must jump directly to game with this balanced 14 count and hearts well-stopped. 3NT, after all, is the bid you should have chosen if the auction had been non-competitive.

(b)   ♠ A 4 3 2   ♡ 6   ◇ 9 8   ♣ A K J 10 5 2

BID 3 ♣. Although you would have bid 1 ♠ over 1 ◇ in a non-competitive auction (since 2 ♣ would have denied a four-card major), you must first bid you fine club suit, which is 100% forcing. Hopefully, you will be able to show your four-card spade suit later. Bid your longer suit first in a competitive auction at high levels.

Do not be pushed into foolish bids at high levels when your opponents pre-empt the bidding immediately. They are often very costly and can have serious effects on partnership confidence and morale. Sometimes you will be "fixed" by your opponents' pre-emptive tactics — accept it. A good example of being goaded into a disastrous contract took place when one of your authors pre-empted on the following deal played in a friendly rubber bridge game:

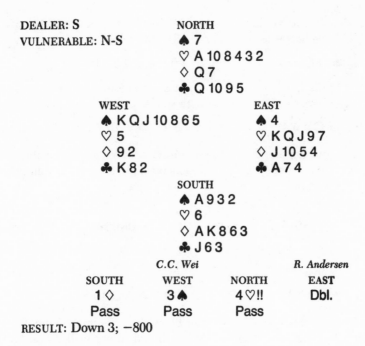

DEALER: S
VULNERABLE: N-S

NORTH
♠ 7
♡ A 10 8 4 3 2
♢ Q 7
♣ Q 10 9 5

WEST
♠ K Q J 10 8 6 5
♡ 5
♢ 9 2
♣ K 8 2

EAST
♠ 4
♡ K Q J 9 7
♢ J 10 5 4
♣ A 7 4

SOUTH
♠ A 9 3 2
♡ 6
♢ A K 8 6 3
♣ J 6 3

	C.C. Wei		*R. Andersen*
SOUTH	WEST	NORTH	EAST
1 ♢	3 ♠	4 ♡ !!	Dbl.
Pass	Pass	Pass	

RESULT: Down 3; −800

North apologized for his lack of discretion but explained that he feared
that the 3 ♠ bid at favorable vulnerability was intended to keep his side
from reaching a heart game. And he wasn't going to be pre-empted out
of a vulnerable game since he could not double 3 ♠. Actually, 3 ♠ would
have been defeated one trick for 50 points; instead, the defense collect-
ed 800 points.

Basically, your approach over jump overcalls should be similar to your
approach over simple overcalls. Raises, NT bids, and new suits suggest
better hands as the level of the bidding is increased. And never forget
what is often your most deadly weapon − the penalty double. Make your
opponents pay (when they are completely out of line) for attempting to
fight cannons with cap pistols! But don't let them push you into foolish
high level bids.

Exercise #7
Handling competition over 1 ◊, 1 ♡, and 1 ♠

Partner opens 1 ◊, and the opponent makes a takeout double. What initial response would you make with the following hands:

1. ♠ Q J 10 7 6
   ♡ 3
   ◊ Q 10 5
   ♣ K 10 3 2

2. ♠ K J 10
   ♡ A Q
   ◊ 10 9 4 2
   ♣ J 10 9 5

3. ♠ K J 10 9
   ♡ K Q 10 7
   ◊ 7
   ♣ K 10 9 8

4. ♠ A 7
   ♡ 9
   ◊ K J 10 9 5 2
   ♣ Q 10 8 7

5. ♠ 9 8 4 2
   ♡ Q 7 6 3
   ◊ 8
   ♣ Q 10 8 5

6. ♠ A J 10 5 4
   ♡ 6
   ◊ 9 8
   ♣ A J 9 8 3

Partner opens 1 ♡ and the opponent makes a takeout double. What initial response would you make with the following hands:

7. ♠ A 8 2
   ♡ K 10 9 5
   ◊ K 10 7 4
   ♣ 8 6

8. ♠ 6 2
   ♡ 8 5
   ◊ A K Q 10 5 4
   ♣ Q 3 2

As responder, what bid would you make in the following auctions:

OPENER	OPPONENT	RESPONDER
1 ◊	1 ♠	?

9. ♠ A Q 9
   ♡ K 4 3
   ◊ Q 5 4 2
   ♣ J 10 8

10. ♠ 10 9 4
    ♡ A K J 3 2
    ◊ 7 5 4
    ♣ 9 6

11. ♠ Q J 9 4 2
    ♡ A 3
    ◊ 5 4
    ♣ A 8 7 2

OPENER	OPPONENT	RESPONDER
1 ♡	2 ♣	?

12. ♠ K Q J 10
    ♡ A 10 9
    ◊ J 10 6 2
    ♣ 8 4

13. ♠ A Q J 10 2
    ♡ 7 5
    ◊ J 5 4 2
    ♣ 5 3

14. ♠ A Q 10
    ♡ 10 7
    ◊ K J 10 9 7 3 2
    ♣ 8

Partner opens 1♡, and the opponent makes a strong 1NT overcall. What initial action would you take with the following hands:

15. ♠ K Q J 10 7	16. ♠ 5 2	17. ♠ 6
♡ 8 7	♡ 7	♡ Q 8 5 2
◇ K 10	◇ J 10 4 2	◇ A J 10 7 3 2
♣ Q 10 9 5	♣ K Q J 10 7 4	♣ J 10

As responder, what bid would you make in the following auctions:

OPENER	OPPONENT	RESPONDER
1♡	2♠	?

18. ♠ 5	19. ♠ A Q	20. ♠ Q J 9 7
♡ K 10 7 3	♡ 10 9	♡ 4
◇ A Q 10 7 6	◇ K 10 9 3 2	◇ A 10 5 3
♣ Q 10 4	♣ A J 10 6	♣ K 10 9 3

OPENER	OPPONENT	RESPONDER
1♠	3♣	?

21. ♠ 8 5	22. ♠ J 10 9 2
♡ K Q 10 9 7	♡ A 10 9
◇ Q 10 7 6	◇ A 10 7 6
♣ J 4	♣ 5 3

OPENER	OPPONENT	RESPONDER
1◇	3♣	?

23. ♠ A K J 10	24. ♠ A 10 7
♡ A Q J 10	♡ A 8 7 3
◇ K J 10 3	◇ 8 7
♣ 2	♣ Q 10 9 2

Answers
Exercise #7

1. 1♠
Make the natural response you would have made in a non-competitive auction.

2. 2NT
Although you have sufficient strength for a redouble, you really have no interest in doubling a low-level contract with this hand. Jump to 2NT describing your balanced 11 count with scattered strength.

3. Redouble
Prospects for a lucrative penalty double are promising. You have excellent defense against any contract your opponents might select.

4. 3◇
Invitational jump raise with excellent trump support. (All raises convey their non-competitive meaning over a takeout double.)

5. Pass
An excellent description.

6. 1♠
Although you have the strength for a re-double, it is best to start bidding your suits. The enemy obviously has a fit in hearts. Remember, the failure to redouble does not limit your strength. All responses are natural.

7. 3♡
Same as a non-competitive jump raise — 11-13 points in support of hearts.

8. 2◇
The response you would have made in a non-competitive auction.

9. 2NT
Natural response you would have made in a non-competitive auction. Obviously, promises spades well-stopped.

10. Pass
Although without the overcall you would have responded 1♡ over 1◇, you must have considerably more strength to introduce your suit freely at the two-level. The bidding is unlikely to die at 1♠, so you hope to be able to show your heart suit subsequently, having limited your strength by your initial pass.

11. Double
Ideal for a penalty double of 1♠.

12. 3♡
Invitational jump raise — 11-13 HCP and a fit for opener's suit.

13. Pass
Although you have sufficient strength to bid 1♠ over 1♡, you cannot bid 2♠ over the 2♣ overcall. Introducing a new suit at the two-level would suggest 11 HCP.

14. 2◇
The call you would have made had your opponent passed 1♡. You only have 10 HCP, but your good seven-card suit compensates for the lack of an additional jack.

15. Double
You have an excellent lead and your side has the balance of strength.

16. 2♣
Not forcing. Remember, with the 11 HCP that are normally required for a two-over-one response, you would have doubled 1NT.

17. 3♡
Invitational jump raise. Suggests a highly distributional jump raise, since if most of your strength was in high cards you would have doubled 1NT.

18. 4♡
With 14 HCP in support of hearts, jump to game.

19. 3NT
You have game-going values and their suit well-stopped.

20. Double
Your hand is perfect for a double of 2♠ on this obvious misfit.

21. Pass
You are far short of a forcing 3♡ call. Don't let the opponents' preempts push you into foolish overbids.

22. 3♠
Your controls and good fit for spades tip the scales in favor of bidding 3♠. Remember, however, this is a *minimum* hand for raising opener's suit at the three level.

23. 4♣
An excellent cue-bid. You are interested in slam, have control in the enemy suit, and are without a good suit to suggest as trump.

24. Double
A sound penalty double on what was likely to yield only a part-score deal for your side.

Chapter 10

Precision's Preemptive Opening Bids

PRECISION'S PREEMPTIVE opening bids are designed to complement its limited opening bids. In addition to cutting down the enemy bidding space, their purpose is to precisely describe useful distributional hands that do not meet the requirements of an opening bid.

So that responder can judge both the offensive and defensive potential of your side, it is necessary to follow certain strict requirements:

(a) Your long suit usually should contain no more than two losers opposite a singleton in partner's hand, assuming normal breaks.

(b) Your hand should not include a four-card major side suit.

(c) Your hand should not include more than one ace or king outside the trump suit.

Although, under special circumstances to be described later, some of these requirements can be relaxed, they are critical in giving responder the ability to accurately determine the best course of action for your side.

In regard to playing strength, there is one standard we apply to all preemptive openings — the "rule of 2 and 3." Simply stated, this rule says:

"Not vulnerable, you are within three tricks of your contract. Vulnerable, you are within two tricks of your contract."

This is an excellent "safety-gauge" when you are considering a preemptive opening. Like the safety gauges in your automobile, it warns you of impending danger.

The word "preemptive" implies weakness, and indeed many of the Precision preemptive opening bids and responses are designed largely to interfere with the opponents' communications. However, they are also designed to reach your side's optimum contract when responder has a good hand. You can have your "cake" and "eat it too" if responder can always count on opener to follow strictly the requirements for the preemptive opening bid he makes.

2♡ and 2♠ openings

2♡ and 2♠ in Precision describe hands with good suits that do not meet the requirements for an opening one-bid. They are commonly called "weak two-bids," opposed to Standard American's "strong two-bids" which describe game-going values in the opener's hand.

The requirements for a Precision 2♡ or 2♠ opening are very specific:

(1) A *good* six-card suit; (at least two of the top four honors.)

(2) 5-10 HCP, with most of the points concentrated in the suit.

(3) A one-suited hand. (You may have a four-card minor, but *never* four cards in the other major.)

Following these guidelines, let's consider a few examples:

(a) ♠ A 10 7 5 3 2   ♡ 6 4   ◊ Q J 10   ♣ 9 8

It would be unwise to open this hand 2♠ for two reasons:

(1) Your spade suit is too weak; and

(2) Your playing strength is inadequate at any vulnerability, because you are not even within three tricks of your bid (rule of 2 and 3).

(b) ♠ J 8 4 2   ♡ A Q 10 9 8 4   ◊ 8 5   ♣ 9

Here the objection to opening 2♡ is your four-card support for spades. You run the risk of preempting *your* side out of a spade contract.

(c) ♠ J 10 9 8 7 6   ♡ A 3   ◊ A 6 2   ♣ J 10

2♠ would be a poor opening bid with this hand since your suit is too weak and most of your strength is located outside of the suit.

(d) ♠ K Q J 10 7 2   ♡ 7   ◊ K 8 7   ♣ 9 8 4

Open 2♠. This hand meets all our requirements for a "weak two-bid."

(e) ♠ 8 6 2   ♡ A J 10 8 7 2   ◊ A 6   ♣ 8 7

Although your suit could be a bit better, this is an acceptable 2♡ opening.

(f) ♠ K Q 10 9 8 5   ♡ 6 2   ◊ Q J   ♣ Q J 10

Despite your 11 HCP this is a 2♠ opening, not a 1♠ opening. 11 point hands that are primarily queens and jacks are without defensive strength and should not be opened with a one-bid. But they can be opened with a two-bid if they contain a good six-card suit.

Responding to 2♡ and 2♠

Since both the strength and nature of opener's hand is clearly defined when he opens 2♡ or 2♠, responder's task is usually quite simple. By using the Limited Bid Strategy he can normally determine your combined assets.

We recommend the following structure of responses:

Over 2♡ or 2♠

(a) Single raise is preemptive — *not* an encouragement or invitation to game.

(b) Jumps to game may be based on game-going values or be preemptive. In either case they are sign-offs.

(c) New suits are forcing one-round and invite opener to raise or show a feature.

(d) 2NT is forcing. It asks the opener to name any singleton or void. Opener raises to 3NT to show a solid six-card suit (AKQxxx or better).

(e) 3NT or jumps to game in new suits are sign-offs, placing the final contract.

Using these methods, with the following hands what would you bid over partner's 2♡ opening?

(a)   ♠ K J 7 3 2   ♡ 4   ◇ K J 8 7   ♣ K J 10

PASS. Game is out of reach and you should not try to improve the contract. Partner has promised a good heart suit, so 2♡ might make with
your outside strength and if opponents compete they court disaster.

(b)   ♠ 8 5   ♡ Q 10 7 2   ◊ A 10 9 7 5 3   ♣ 7

JUMP to 4♡. Pre-empt your opponents to the limit with your excellent
trump support and good distribution. Your opponents must have game
in either spades or clubs, and your 4♡ bid may prevent them from
getting together. Remember, from their point of view you may have
jumped to 4♡ with a good hand. Your left-hand opponent may give you
credit for the high cards that are actually held by his partner.

(c)   ♠ A 8 6 5   ♡ Q 10 5   ◊ A K 10   ♣ 9 8 4

BID 2NT, asking partner if he has any singleton or voids. Game is
possible if partner is short in clubs. You have a good fit for hearts and 3♡
should be safe in any event. If partner rebids 3♡ we would pass, and
over 3 ◊ we would simply return to 3♡. Partner is permitted to carry on
to game with an absolute maximum after a 2NT response and
subsequent return to three of his suit.

In the following examples partner has opening 2♠. What would you
bid?

(d)   ♣ 6 4   ♡ A K Q J 10 7 3   ◊ K 4   ♣ J 10

BID 4♡. Sign-off by bidding what you think you can make.

(e)   ♠ 9 8   ♡ A Q J 10 9 5   ◊ A J 7   ♣ K 4

BID 3♡. Introducing a new suit is absolutely forcing and invites partner
to raise. If partner rebids 3♠, we would raise to 4♠.

A 2NT response is frequently very helpful in reaching good game and
slam contracts that depend on a good fit readily located when opener
reveals shortness in a side suit. Consider this deal from a Team event
played in Chicago.

DEALER: S
VULNERABLE: E-W

NORTH
♠ K J 5
♡ A K Q J 6
◇ 9 8 3
♣ A 4

WEST
♠ 8 7
♡ 10 9 3
◇ A Q J 5 2
♣ K 8 2

EAST
♠ 6 4
♡ 5 4 2
◇ K 10 7 4
♣ Q J 7 6

SOUTH
♠ A Q 10 9 3 2
♡ 8 7
◇ 6
♣ 10 9 5 3

SOUTH	WEST	NORTH	EAST
2♠	Pass	2NT¹	Pass
3◇²	Dbl.³	4NT⁴	Pass
5◇⁵	Pass	6♠	Pass
Pass	Pass		

RESULT: Making 6

¹ Conventional forcing response asking for shortness.
² Singleton or void in diamonds.
³ Lead-directing double in the event partner should be on lead against the final contract. Excellent tactic.
⁴ Blackwood.
⁵ One ace.

This fine 24 point slam contributed substantially to the Precision team winning a close match. The key was locating the shortness in diamonds.

In addition to reaching good game and slam contracts, 2NT will often prevent you from reaching hopeless contracts when the hands do not fit. Suppose opener rebids 3♣ after your 2NT response to 2♠. You hold:

♠ J 10 4   ♡ K 7 5   ◇ 9 8 4 2   ♣ A K Q

You should quietly retreat to 3♠ and hope partner doesn't have an absolute maximum and raise to 4♠, because you fear several diamond losers. However, if partner were to bid 3◇ over your 2NT inquiry, you would happily and confidently bid 4♠.

Using the guidelines and principles we have discussed, 2 ♡ and 2 ♠ openings can be a valuable tool in your Precision arsenal, both offensively and defensively.

3 ♣ and 3 ◇ openings

Precision 3 ♣ and 3 ◇ openings are more constructive in nature than a standard preemptive three-bid. Like 2 ♡ and 2 ♠ openings, they describe a very specific hand. The requirements are:

(1) A semi-solid seven-card suit — at least two of the top three honors.

(2) An outside entry — usually ace or king.

(3) 8 to 10 HCP.

Using these standards, let's examine a few hands with which you might consider opening 3 ♣ or 3 ◇:

(a) ♠ J 7 6 3   ♡ A   ◇ K Q 10 9 8 5 4   ♣ 6

You should not open this hand 3 ◇ since you have a four-card major. Your hand would make an excellent dummy for a spade contract, and 3 ◇ could easily prevent your side from locating a spade fit.

(b) ♠ K 7   ♡ 9 8   ◇ 10 7   ♣ A J 9 7 6 4 2

Here the objection to a 3 ♣ opening is the quality of your club suit. 3 ♣ would imply a far better club suit.

(c) ♠ Q J 10   ♡ 5   ◇ 10 9   ♣ A Q J 10 9 7 4

Although we would prefer the ♠ K, in place of the ♠ Q-J-10, this hand meets all the requirements for a Precision 3 ♣ opening. You want to invite partner to bid 3NT, while, if partner has a poor hand, you have taken two levels of bidding from your opponents.

(d) ♠ 7 5   ♡ A 4   ◇ Q 10 9 6 5 3 2   ♣ A 7

Never open 3 ◇ with this type of hand. Your suit is far too weak and you have too much outside strength.

(e) ♠ A 6   ♡ 9 6   ◇ K Q J 9 8 5 4   ♣ 3 2

Open 3 ◊. You have a fine seven-card diamond suit and the required outside entry.

Responding to 3 ♣ and 3 ◊

In addition to accepting the obvious invitation to bid 3NT, responder has several possible courses of action when partner opens 3 ♣ or 3 ◊. The following box outlines the methods we recommend:

Over 3 ♣ and 3 ◊

(1) Single raise is defensive — *not* an encouragement or invitation to game.

(2) Jumps to game may be either preemptive or with game-going values unsuited for 3NT.

(3) 3 ♡ and 3 ♠ are forcing one-round and show a good five-card or longer suit. Opener is invited to raise on honor doubleton or xxx. Lacking a fit for responder's suit, opener can either show his outside entry if convenient, or rebid his suit.

(4) 3NT and jumps to game are sign-offs; opener must pass.

(5) Over 3 ♣, 3 ◊ is conventional, asking opener for the location of his outside entry. Opener rebids:

3 ♡ = heart entry; 3 ♠ = spade entry; 3NT = diamond entry.

Using these methods, what would you respond to partner's 3 ♣ opening with these hands?

(a) ♠ 10 9 8 4   ♡ J 6 5 4   ◊ A K J   ♣ J 7

PASS. 3NT and 5 ♣ are both out of reach even if opener has a maximum 3 ♣ opener. You have reasonable defensive strength, so there is no reason to raise preemptively to the four level.

(b) ♠ A K Q 10 6 2   ♡ A 10 9   ◊ 6   ♣ J 10 4

BID 3 ♠. Either 4 ♠ or 5 ♣ should provide an excellent game contract for your side. 3 ♠ is forcing and opener's rebid will clarify which game your side should bid. (You intend to pass 4 ♠ and bid 5 ♣ over any other rebid.)

(c)   ♠ 9 8 4   ♡ A J 10 8   ◇ A K 9 3   ♣ 7 4

Use the conventional 3 ◇ response to locate your side's best contract. If opener rebids 3 ♠, we would sign-off in 3NT. A 3 ♡ or 3NT rebid (showing a diamond feature) will inform responder that the partnership does not have a spade stopper, eliminating 3NT as a final contract. You should then content yourself with 5 ♣.

Should partner open 3 ◇, how would you respond with the following hands?

(d)   ♠ J 10 5 4   ♡ A 8 7 6   ◇ K 8   ♣ A 6 3

3NT should be a claim despite your side's holding of only 21 or 22 HCP. (You can plan on seven diamond winners, your two aces, and partner's side value will simply be an overtrick.)

(e)   ♠ A 4   ♡ K Q J 10 9 7 5   ◇ 10 9   ♣ K 3

JUMP to 4 ♡. Bid what you think you can make. Partner has two of the top three diamond honors and an outside feature which should provide you with 10 winners and protect you from more than three losers. There is no reason to bid a forcing 3 ♡ since you need no support for your fine suit.

The last two examples illustrate the importance of counting tricks, not points, in responding to partner's preemptive opening. Points, as we noted in Chapter 1, don't take tricks; and counting them will not always give you an accurate prediction of your side's trick-taking potential, particularly when partner has shown a good long suit.

Four and five level minor suit openings 4 ♣, 4 ◇, 5 ♣, 5 ◇

Opening 4 ♣ or 4 ◇ describes a reasonable eight-card broken suit with little outside strength. Assuming normal breaks, the opener should expect to win seven tricks if he is not vulnerable and eight tricks vulnerable. (The rule of 2 and 3.) No more than one of these tricks should be located outside the trump suit. Generally, it is best if your hand contains no voids when you open 4 ♣ or 4 ◇.

Not vulnerable, open either of the following hands with a four-level minor suit pre-empt:

(a) ♠ 6 5   ♡ 5   ◇ 9 6   ♣ A Q 10 9 7 6 4 2

Open 4♣. We expect to win seven tricks in the club suit assuming normal distribution.

(b) ♠ 8   ♡ 9 8 4   ◇ K Q 10 9 7 5 4 3   ♣ J

Open 4 ◇. Prospects for seven tricks are reasonable even if partner has a useless hand.

Vulnerable, you should have a better hand to commit your side to the four-level. For example:

(c) ♠ K 7   ♡ 7 6   ◇ 8   ♣ A Q 10 9 6 4 3 2

Open 4♣. It is acceptable to have one potential trick outside your suit. You can reasonably expect to win eight tricks with this hand.

(d) ♠ 8   ♡ 6   ◇ A Q J 9 8 6 5 2   ♣ Q 10 9

Open 4 ◇. Your suit is excellent and justifies a four-level opening. Assuming the opponents compete, they may find it difficult to reach their better major suit contract.

Opening 5♣ or 5 ◇ is simply a matter of one additional trick. You need a minimum of eight prospective winners not vulnerable and nine tricks vulnerable. The additional trick should come from either a better or longer trump suit.

We would open 5♣, not vulnerable, holding:

♠ 5   ♡ 8   ◇ Q J 10   ♣ A K 10 9 7 4 3 2

Vulnerable, we would open 5 ◇ with:

♠ A 7   ♡ 5   ◇ K Q J 8 7 5 4 3 2   ♣ 8.

The key to high-level preemptive bids is the number of tricks you are likely to win with your suit as trump. It is your "safety gauge" and gives responder a clear picture of your side's defensive and offensive potential.

Responding to 4♣, 4◇, 5♣, & 5◇

Responder rarely has more than two choices in responding to a high-level minor suit pre-empt: (1) PASS: (2) RAISE. The reason is simple. Opener's hand is likely to be completely worthless unless his suit is trump.

Therefore, we advise the simple approach outlined in the following box:

Over 4♣ and 4◇

1. 4♡ & 4♠: sign-off. (Despite opener's warning that his hand may be worthless without his suit as trump.)
   5♣/4◇ & 5◇/4♣

2. 4NT: Blackwood = asking for aces.

3. Game bids are either based on game-going values or are preemptive.

4. 4◇ over 4♣ is conventional, asking opener to show a short suit. Opener rebids:
   4♡ = shortness in hearts; 4♠ = shortness in spades; 4NT = shortness in diamonds.
   With shortness in more than one suit, opener shows hearts first, spades next (denying hearts), and finally diamonds (via 4NT which denies both heart and spade shortness).

Using these responses, what action would you take over partner's minor suit pre-empt with the following:

(a) Partner opens 4♣ vulnerable:

♠ K J 10 5 3 2   ♡ K Q 9 8   ◇ Q J 5   ♣ –

PASS. "Don't jump out of the frying pan into the fire!" Partner has a good, long club suit at this vulnerability and your high cards should provide a trick or two. Remember, opener's hand may be totally worthless for playing at spades.

(b) Partner opens 4◇ not vulnerable:

♠ 6   ♡ 9 8 5 3   ◇ K 5 2   ♣ A 10 9 7 4

BID 5 ◇. Your opponents must have at least a game in one of the major suits. The raise to 5 ◇ may prevent them from getting together and should not prove costly, even if you are doubled. Indeed, with luck 5 ◇ may make.

(c)   Partner opens 4 ♣ not vulnerable:

♠ A K Q 10 9 8 5   ♡ Q J 10 8   ◇ –   ♣ J 6

BID 4 ♠. A rare situation where responder should disregard opener's warning and play game in his own suit.

(d)   Partner opens 4 ◇ vulnerable:

♠ A 8 5 2   ♡ K 9 5   ◇ Q 3   ♣ A 9 8 5

BID 5 ◇. Your hand is likely to provide three tricks. Added to partner's eight tricks at this vulnerability, prospects for game are excellent.

(e)   Partner opens 4 ♣ vulnerable:

♠ A K Q 7   ♡ 9 8 4   ◇ A K 7   ♣ K 3 2

BID 4 ◇. An excellent opportunity to find out if opener is short in hearts, which is all that this hand requires for slam.

(f)   Partner open 5 ◇ not vulnerable:

♠ A Q 10 9 7 4 2   ♡ A 8 5 2   ◇ –   ♣ Q 6

PASS. Partner has eight winners with diamonds as trump. You have at least two winners which means your side may well make 5 ◇. Don't consider bidding 5 ♠.

As these hands illustrate, when partner makes a high-level minor suit preemptive opening the number of points you hold is not nearly as important as the number of tricks you can contribute and the number of losers you can prevent.

Major suit preemptive openings 3 ♡, 3 ♠, 4 ♡, 4 ♠

High-level major suit preemptive openings are similar to minor suit pre-empts. The key to success with them is the Rule of 2 and 3.

Opening 3 ♡ or 3 ♠ describes a good seven-card suit with little outside strength. The opener should expect to win six tricks if he is not vulnerable and seven tricks vulnerable. Most, if not all, of these tricks should come from opener's long suit. It is also best if opener's hand contains no voids when he opens 3 ♡ or 3 ♠.

Not vulnerable, we would open 3 ♡ holding:

(a)   ♠ 6   ♡ Q J 10 9 8 7 3   ◊ K 10 9   ♣ 8 7

or

(b)   ♠ 6 4   ♡ K Q 10 9 8 5 4   ◊ 9   ♣ Q J 10

Vulnerable, you must be a trick stronger. You might open 3 ♠ with either:

(c)   ♠ A Q J 10 8 7 3   ♡ 6 5   ◊ K 10 8   ♣ 7

or

(d)   ♠ K Q J 9 8 6 4   ♡ 3   ◊ A 4   ♣ 8 7 5

However, you should not open three of a major with either of the following hands:

(e)   ♠ 10 9 5 2   ♡ A Q J 10 9 7 5   ◊ J   ♣ 10

Never open 3 ♡ holding four spades.

(f)   ♠ J 10 9 8 6 5 2   ♡ A 6 3   ◊ K 5 4   ♣ –

In addition to your void, the spade suit is too weak to consider opening 3 ♠ and you have far too much outside strength.

As with most other Precision pre-empts, there are no point count requirements for opening 3 ♡ or 3 ♠. It is strictly a matter of playing strength concentrated in your long suit.

Opening 4 ♡ or 4 ♠, instead of 3 ♡ or 3 ♠ is simply a matter of one more trick. The additional trick should usually come from a better or longer trump suit. Most 4 ♡ or 4 ♠ openings contain an eight-card trump suit. Keep in mind you are more likely to be doubled when you open at the game level. There is less risk in doubling a game than a part-score. Open 4 ♡ not vulnerable with:

♠ 4   ♡ A K J 10 9 6 5 2   ◇ 10 9 4   ♣ 8

Open 4 ♠ vulnerable holding:

♠ A Q J 10 7 6 4 3   ♡ 2   ◇ K 10 9   ♣ 6.

By closely following these requirements and standards, responder will be in an excellent position to judge your side's defensive and offensive potential. Deviating from them will place responder in an impossible position.

Responding to 3 ♡, 3 ♠, 4 ♡, & 4 ♠

Responding to a high-level major suit pre-empt is usually a simple matter of adding your quick tricks *and controls* to the number of playing tricks promised by partner's opening. You should bend over backwards to play in opener's suit, since his hand may be totally worthless if the hand is played elsewhere.

Consider a few examples:

(a)   Partner opens 3 ♡ not vulnerable. You hold:

♠ K Q 7 3   ♡ J 4   ◇ K Q J 6   ♣ Q J 2

PASS. Don't be influenced by your point count. We would feel fortunate if partner managed to score nine tricks with hearts as trump, let along ten. And you should not consider bidding 3NT. Remember, partner said he could win six tricks only if hearts were trump.

(b)   Partner opens 3 ♠ vulnerable. You hold:

♠ Q   ♡ A K 5   ◇ A 10 9 2   ♣ J 10 7 3 2

RAISE to 4 ♠. Partner believes he can win seven tricks with spades as trump. You have three quick tricks plus the queen of trump which should solidify partner's suit.

We have no special tools or gadgets to suggest over major suit pre-empts. For the most part they are not needed. Using the Limited Bid Strategy based on TRICKS, not points, responder should be able to set the final contract directly. Opener, having limited his hand very precisely, should respect any decision responder makes.

Before we consider Exercise # 8, one word of warning to the player who opens the bidding with a preemptive call. When you have opened the bidding with a pre-empt, you have told your complete story: DO NOT REPEAT YOURSELF. Once a player preempts he should not bid again, unless partner forces him to do so.

Exercise #8
Preemptive openings & responses

Not vulnerable, what opening bid would you make with the following hands?

1. ♠ K J 10 9 4 2
   ♡ 10 9 7 5
   ♢ A 6
   ♣ 7

2. ♠ Q J 10 9 7 5 4
   ♡ K 3
   ♢ A 9 4
   ♣ 6

3. ♠ A 6
   ♡ 7
   ♢ K Q J 8 7 4 2
   ♣ 9 8 3

4. ♠ 9
   ♡ K Q 10 6 4 3
   ♢ K 10 7
   ♣ 10 9 4

5. ♠ A Q J 10 8 6 3
   ♡ 4
   ♢ 3
   ♣ Q J 10 5

6. ♠ 5
   ♡ 8 7
   ♢ K Q J 7 6 4 3 2
   ♣ 9 5

Vulnerable, what opening bid would you make with the following hands?

7. ♠ A 5
   ♡ K Q J 9 5 2
   ♢ 10 9 4
   ♣ 7 4

8. ♠ 6
   ♡ 3
   ♢ A K 10 9 6 5 3 2
   ♣ Q J 7

9. ♠ A K J 10 9 5 3 2
   ♡ 3
   ♢ 9
   ♣ Q 10 9

10. ♠ 6 5
    ♡ Q J 10 9 6 3 2
    ♢ K 4 2
    ♣ 8

11. ♠ K 10
    ♡ 5 2
    ♢ 10 9
    ♣ A Q J 9 7 6 3

12. ♠ 7
    ♡ A Q J 10 6 5 2
    ♢ Q J 10
    ♣ 8 5

As responder, what would you bid in the following auctions (vulnerability given)?

OPENER	RESPONDER	(Vulnerable)
2♡	?	

13. ♠ A K 6
    ♡ J 7 3
    ♢ 9 8 4 2
    ♣ K Q 10

14. ♠ Q 9 8 6 4 3
    ♡ 2
    ♢ A J 10 3 2
    ♣ 4

15. ♠ 6 4
    ♡ Q 9 5
    ♢ A 10 6 3 2
    ♣ K 10 9

	OPENER	RESPONDER	(Vulnerable)
	3♣	?	

16. ♠ A 10 9 2
    ♡ 7 6 3
    ◇ A Q 10 5
    ♣ K 7

17. ♠ 7 2
    ♡ 8 5 2
    ◇ A 10 9 5 3
    ♣ Q 6 2

18. ♠ 6 5
    ♡ A K Q 10 7
    ◇ A 7 5 2
    ♣ K 8

	OPENER	RESPONDER	(Not Vulnerable)
	3♠	?	

19. ♠ J
    ♡ A 10 7 6
    ◇ A K 8 5
    ♣ K 5 4 2

20. ♠ –
    ♡ K Q 10 7 6 3 2
    ◇ Q 6 3
    ♣ K 10 7

	OPENER	RESPONDER	(Not Vulnerable)
	4♣	?	

21. ♠ A K 7 6 2
    ♡ 9 8 3
    ◇ A K 10 4
    ♣ K

22. ♠ 8 3
    ♡ A 5
    ◇ K 10 9 7 3 2
    ♣ Q 9 5

As opener, what would your rebid be in the following auctions?

OPENER	RESPONDER
2♠	2NT
?	

23. ♠ A K Q 10 7 3
    ♡ 6 5
    ◇ 9 8
    ♣ 7 5 2

24. ♠ A K 10 9 4 3
    ♡ 4
    ◇ Q 10 7
    ♣ 10 9 6

OPENER	RESPONDER
3♣	3◇
?	

25. ♠ K 6
    ♡ 9 4 2
    ◇ 7
    ♣ A Q 10 9 5 3 2

26. ♠ 8 5
    ♡ A 9
    ◇ 8 7
    ♣ K Q 10 9 7 5 4

27.	OPENER	RESPONDER		28.	OPENER	RESPONDER
	3 ♠	3NT			4 ♣	4 ♦
	?				?	

♠ Q J 10 7 6 4 2
♡ 7
♦ 4
♣ Q J 10 9

♠ 5
♡ K 10
♦ 8 2
♣ A Q J 8 7 5 4 2

29.	OPENER	RESPONDER
	4 ♦	4 ♠
	?	

♠ —
♡ 10 9 4
♦ A K 10 9 5 4 3 2
♣ K 2

Answers
Exercise #8

1. Pass
Although your suit and general strength meet the requirements for a 2 ♠ opening, you should never open 2 ♡ or 2 ♠ with four cards in the other major.

2. Pass
You have too much strength outside your suit to open 3 ♠. Remember, you should have no more than one outside trick when you make a preemptive opening.

3. 3 ♦
A perfect description of your semi-solid seven card suit and outside entry.

4. 2 ♡
Perfectly acceptable weak two-bid not vulnerable.

5. 4 ♠
The four-card club suit to the contrary, the spade suit and playing strength are excellent for a 4 ♠ opening.

6. 4 ♦
Minimum values for a 4 ♦ opening. You are within three tricks of your contract not vulnerable assuming a normal break of the outstanding diamonds.

7. 2 ♡
Sound vulnerable weak two-bid.

8. 4 ♦
You have reasonable expectations of winning eight tricks with diamonds as trumps.

9. 4 ♠
A minimum 4 ♠ opening vulnerable.

10. Pass
Too weak for a vulnerable 3 ♡ opening.

11. 3 ♣
Describing your semi-solid seven-card suit with an outside entry.

12. 3 ♡
You have a fine suit and expect to win a minimum of seven tricks, even if partner holds a worthless hand.

13. 2NT
Asking opener to show a short side-suit if he has one or raise to 3NT with solid hearts. If partner has shortness in diamonds, game at hearts is more than likely.

14. Pass

Do not try to "improve" the contract. Remember, both 2 ♠ and 3 ◇ by you would be 100% forcing, and you certainly don't want to drive the bidding higher on this probable misfit. Partner must have a reasonable heart suit at this vulnerability.

15. 3 ♡

Preemptive raise. Your opponents have a good spade fit and 3 ♡ should not be an unreasonable contract with your fine fit and moderate strength.

16. 3 ◇

Asking partner to show his side entry. If his outside strength is in hearts, your side should have a good play for 3NT.

17. 4 ♣

Preemptive raise. Your opponents must have a good fit in one, if not both, major suits and probably the values for game. Make it more difficult for them to get together by jacking up the bidding to the four-level.

18. 3 ♡

100% forcing and partner's rebid should clarify where this hand should be played. If partner raises hearts, you will pass. Should he bid 3 ♠, revealing a spade entry, rebid 3NT. And over 4 ♣, raise to 5 ♣.

19. 4 ♠

Opener has promised he can win six tricks with spades as trump; add the four tricks your hand could easily produce and game is more than possible. Singleton jack is adequate support for a good seven-card suit.

20. Pass

Do not consider "correcting" 3 ♠ to 4 ♡. Opener's hand might be totally worthless in a heart contract. Hopefully, your high cards may be of some value to partner playing 3 ♠.

21. 4 ◇

Asking partner to show a short side-suit. You do not intend to play less than 5 ♣ with your excellent hand, and we would jump to 6 ♣ if partner is short in hearts.

22. 5 ♣

Preemptive raise. Your opponents must have game in one of the majors. 5 ♣ rates to be an economical sacrifice, and bidding it directly may even prevent your opponents from doubling. On a lucky day partner might have the perfect hand and 5 ♣ would be unbreakable.

23. 3NT

Describing your solid spade suit.

24. 3 ♡

Showing your singleton heart.

25. 3 ♠

Informing partner that your entry is in spades.

26. 3 ♡

Revealing your heart entry.

27. Pass

Partner has set the final contract despite your warning that your hand may be totally worthless unless spades are trump. Show faith.

28. 4 ♠

4 ◇ over 4 ♣ asks opener to show shortness in a side-suit.

29. Pass

Same as (27). Partner has placed the final contract. Despite your void in trump, you should have a fairly useful hand for partner.

summary

BRIDGE IS A PARTNERSHIP GAME and the best way for any pair to improve its skill is by thoroughly understanding its agreed methods. The principles suggested in this book have worked for World and National Champions and they can work for you, whether you are playing in a friendly social game, perhaps with your spouse as your partner, or in the tough competition of high-stake bridge or tournaments.

When you play Precision with a regular partner, you will enjoy many advantages. Some of these are bound to impress other players in your game and you may find them eager to adopt a few of the Precision ideas which can easily be grafted onto standard methods: for instance, the 1 ♣ opening to show a strong hand; the 2 ◊ bid to show a three suiter with void or singleton in diamonds; the use of five-card majors; the 13-15 HCP notrump which helps you to avoid the problem of which suit to bid when you have two four-carders; the weak two-bid in the majors, etc. And you will find your partnership results improving dramatically with each of these bids you get them to try.

Should you, yourself, find some of the methods a bit too complicated for easy recall at the table, by all means eliminate those suggestions from your partnership. Remember, Precision is like a menu in a fine restaurant. You are invited to pick and choose those items that are most likely to work for you.

Bidding systems alone, however, cannot make you a winner at the bridge table. They cannot develop good judgment or sound partnerships. Nor can they improve your opening leads, declarer play, or defense. This you must do yourself. These suggestions might prove helpful:

1. PLAY.   The best way to improve your bridge game is by playing. The better the competition, the more you are likely to learn.

2. READ.   This is also an excellent vehicle for adding to your knowledge and understanding as well as to your enjoyment of the game. In addition to a number of fine books on various aspects of bidding, there are several fine books on play and defense. * Magazines, newspaper columns, and bridge periodicals are also informative, enjoyable and relatively inexpensive.

3. PRACTICE (A) With only two players
             Many partnerships fail to use this valuable tool in

---

*Especially my co-author's excellent "Goren on Play and Defense. (Doubleday) C. C. W.

improving their bridge game. We recommend the following:

1. Partners (one pair only) practice bidding without interference by dealing out two 13-card hands:
   (a) 1 ♣ openings: Remove four small cards from each suit. Bid as partners.
   (b) Limited openings: Remove three small cards each from ♣ and ◇ suits; deal two hands; bid them as partners.
   (c) Distributional hands: Deal two hands 5-5-3 at a time from an unshuffled deck.
   (d) 2 ♣ and 2 ◇ openings: Remove five small cards from each major suit; deal two hands; bid them as partners.

   NOTE: If you play the Precision 2 ◇ opening showing shortness in diamonds and the other three suits, remove 7 diamonds from the deck and follow the same procedure.

(B) In a four-hand game.
1. For competitive bidding, invite two friends to help give you bidding practice. Deal as in regular rubber bridge and bid competitively. After bidding, examine the hands (do not play) and correct misunderstandings or errors. (This is an excellent preface to a social evening of bridge.)

4. REVIEW.   After a bridge session (or during one if it is convenient and appropriate) examine poor results to find out what went wrong. The purpose of such reviews is not to attach blame to one partner or the other but rather to determine how to avoid similar disasters in the future.

These suggestions will not necessarily make you a winner every time you play. But by following them, improving your concentration, and giving every deal your undivided attention, you will improve your partnership results.

Many partnerships alibi their failure to improve by saying they play only to have fun or a good time. We could not agree more heartily that you should have a good time whenever you play. However, frequent partnership misunderstandings — playing at the one or two-level when you are lay-down for game or slam, or reaching hopeless game or slam contracts — do NOT add to anyone's enjoyment at the bridge table except your opponents'.

Precision is designed to eliminate partnership misunderstandings, thereby improving your results as well as increasing your enjoyment at the bridge table.

Our last suggestion — the most difficult for many bridge players to learn — should be the easiest. BE A GOOD PARTNER. Bridge is first and foremost a partnership game. You automatically have two opponents at the bridge table, don't make a third out of the player sitting across the table from you. Helen Sobel, perhaps the greatest woman player of all time, was known in bridge circles not only as a great player but also as a great partner. Many times she was overheard saying to a partner who had just made a catastrophic blunder in the bidding or play, "Forget it partner, let's play the next hand. I'm sure what you did seemed like a good idea at the time." All partnerships could profit from her excellent example and sound advice. The Golden Rule has its place at the bridge table also.

There are many more refinements to the Precision System that you can add when you have mastered the fundamentals presented in this book. For suggestions of available literature, write to the Precision Club, 277 Park Ave., New York, NY 10017. Meanwhile, if you have absorbed the ideas presented in this introduction of Precision methods for home players and tournament newcomers, you will find this book of real profit to your understanding and enjoyment of the game.